Medjugorje

concise & comprehensive

a pilgrim´s guide

Orsolya Eden

Imprint:

*Orsolya Eden**
c/o AutorenServices.de
Birkenallee 24
36037 Fulda
Germany

* Please don´t send any parcels to this address.
If you would like to send a parcel to me, please enquire first via e - mail for a separate address.
Thank you for your understanding.

E - mail: Orsolyaeden1@use.startmail.com

Cover design, illustration and photos: Orsolya Eden
Translation: Orsolya Eden
Note: Orsolya Eden is a pen name.
ISBN paperback: 978-3-9821154-6-7
Revised edition

Content

Pages

PREFACE — 9

WHAT IS MEDJUGORJE ABOUT? — 10 - 12

THE CORE MESSAGE
(derived from various messages) — 12 - 13

- Call to confession
- Call to prayer
- Call to fasting
- Attendance of Holy Mass
- Lecture of the Holy Bible

PROMINENT MESSAGES — 13 - 24

THE TEN SECRETS — 24 - 27

PILGRIM STATIONS IN MEDJUGORJE — 27 - 51

1.   **Apparition Hill (Podbrdo) and Blue Cross** — 27 - 32

2.   **St. James Church** — 33 - 35

3.   **Križevac - Cross Mountain** — 36 - 38

4.   **The Via Domini** — 39 - 40

5.   **The Statue of the Risen Christ** — 40 - 42

6.   **The House of the Unborn Life** — 42 - 43

7.   **Kovačica Cemetery** — 43 - 44

8.   **Adoration Chapel** — 44

9.   **Candle Park** — 44 - 45

10.   **(Social) Institutions** — 45 - 47

11.   **The Garden of St. Francis** — 48 - 49

12.   **Communities** — 50 - 51

THE VISIONARIES — 52 - 55

1.   **Ivanka Ivanković - Elez** — 52

2.   **Vicka Ivanović - Mijatović** — 52

3.   **Mirjana Dragicević - Soldo** — 52 - 53

4.   **Ivan Dragicević** — 53

5.   **Ivan Ivanković** — 54

6.   **Milka Pavlović** — 54

7.   **Marija Pavlović - Lunetti** — 54

8.   **Jakov Čolo** — 54 - 55

9.   **Jelena Vasilj - Valente** — 55

10.   **Marijana Vasilj - Juricić** — 55

STATEMENT OF THE CHURCH 55 - 57

HOW TO GET TO MEDJUGORJE? 57 - 58

POSSIBLE CONTACT TO THE VISIONARIES 58 - 61

RELEVANT YOU TUBE VIDEOS 61 - 63

SUBJECT - RELATED DVDS 63

BOOKS ABOUT MEDJUGORJE 64 - 66

MEDJUGORJE - MUSIC 66

PRAYERS 66 - 77

1. **The Hail Mary** 66 - 67
2. **The Lord´s Prayer** 67
3. **The Glory be to the Father** 67
4. **The Apostles´ Creed** 67 - 68
5. **The Holy Rosary** 68 - 73
6. **Oh my Jesus** 74
7. **Fatima - Prayer, as transmitted by the Angel of Peace** 74
8. **The Medjugorje Chaplet** 74 - 75
9. **The Chaplet of Divine Mercy** 75 - 76

10.	Consecration Prayer to the Most Holy Trinity through Mother Mary	76 - 77

PRAYER PROGRAMME 78 - 79

EXCURSIONS 79 - 94

1.	Šurmanci - Jesus of Divine Mercy	79 - 81
2.	Our Lady of Tihaljina	82 - 83
3.	Koćuša Waterfalls	83 - 84
4.	Humac - Museum and St. Anthony - Monastery	84 - 86
5.	Mostar	86 - 87
6.	Blagaj Tekke, (a Dervish monastery)	87 - 88
7.	The Kravice Waterfalls	89
8.	Pocitelj	89 - 90
9.	The Nature Reserve Hutovo Blato	90 - 92
10.	Prehistoric grave stele and the village Paoča	93
11.	Die Vjetrenica - Grotto	93
12.	Titos´ Bunker in Konij	94
13.	River-Rafting on the Neretva River	94

MATTERS WORTH KNOWING   95 - 116

1.   **Parish office of St. James**   95

2.   **Information centre "MIR"**   95

3.   **The Information Desk**   95

4.   **Translation of the Holy Mass**   95 - 96
      by radio

5.   **Radio "MIR" Medjugorje**   96

6.   **Bookshop "MIR"**   96

7.   **Bookshop „Les Editions Sakramento"**   96 - 97

8.   **German - Christian Bookshop**   97 - 98
      "Tiberias"

9.   **International Book-, Ssouvenir Shop**   98
      "Devotions"

10.   **Medical care**   98 - 99

11.   **Pharmacies (Ljekarna)**   99 - 100

12.   **Bus station**   101

13.   **Taxis**   101 - 102

14.   **Organised excursions**   103

15.   **Shopping**   103 - 104

16.   **Post offices**   104 - 105

17.   **Parking Lot**   106

18.   **Miracles of the sun: Caution!!!**   106

19.   **Restaurants**   106 - 107

20.   **Fasting**   107

21.   **Confessing in your mother tongue**   107

22.	**Donations**	108
23.	**Registration for pilgrim groups**	108
24.	**Hotels**	108 - 113
25.	**Human outlook**	113
26.	**Site plan**	114 - 115
27.	**Local map**	116

PREFACE

To all who want to give God a try

There it was, this discomfort, this emotion which changes the colour of your face; this feeling of having missed out. In short, I was annoyed. But could I even afford to have this feeling in the information centre at such a holy place like Medjugorje? Probably not. So, I swallowed my frustration, when a friendly lady handed me a city map I couldn´t make much use of. This happened at the beginning of my pilgrimage. Unfortunately, this emotion passed me by a couple more times during my five - day pilgrimage.

I had gone through great lengths to get to this place, where Our Lady appears since 1981. In no way, had I thought that it could be difficult to find my way around without a tour guide. Needless to say, I had prepared myself to the best of my capabilities. But except for the official website, a used pilgrim guide of an Irish pilgrim group and a few You Tube videos, I hadn´t come up with a lot of worthwhile information. On site, it was really difficult to locate the "main" sights between all the souvenir shops. In order to spare you, dear reader, this rummaging, I am writing this little pilgrim guide.

I would like to note, that it is only my aim to provide comprehensive information to everyone who is interested in the phenomenon of Medjugorje. Under no circumstances do I seek to criticise.

WHAT IS MEDJUGORJE ABOUT?

Medjugorje was a rural village with about 2500 inhabitants[1] at the beginning of the 20th century. Today, Medjugorje is a place of pilgrimage, which is visited by about 2.5 million pilgrims from all over the world every year.[2] The population has grown up to 4000 inhabitants.[3] It all started on 24 June 1981. On this day, Our Lady appeared to 6 children in the small village "Bijakovići" near Medjugorje. The apparition took place on a hill. This hill is called Podbrdo (Apparition Hill). The children said that the Virgin Mary appeared to them at around 6:00 p.m. At that time, Medjugorje was still part of communist Yugoslavia.

The names of the visionary children on 24 June 1981 are: Ivanka Ivanković, Vicka Ivanković, Mirjana Dragicević, Ivan Dragićević, Ivan Ivanković and Milka Pavlović. At the subsequent apparition on 25 June 1981, Ivan Ivanković and Milka Pavlović are not present. In their place the Virgin Mary, also called Gospa, is witnessed by two other children. Their names are Marija Pavlović and Jakov Čolo. Jakov Čolo was only ten years old at the time.[4] The Mother of God continues to appear to some of these visionaries up to the present day. It is remarkable that the area of Medjugorje has been inhabited by Christians for 1300 years. The community of Medjugorje itself, was founded in 1892. It was dedicated to St. James, the protector of pilgrims.

---

[1] Franjo Sušac (text and photo), Conect Mostar (and design), *Medjugorje MONOGRAFIA PER I PELLEGRINI,* Grafotisak, Grude 2014, page 6.

[2] ERZDIÖZESE WIEN, Franziskus skeptisch zu neuen Medjugorje-Erscheinungen, in Katholische Kirche Erzdiözese Wien 15. Mai.2017, under: https://www.erzdioezese-wien.at/site/nachrichtenmagazin/schwerpunkt/papstfranziskus/article/57124.html (retrieved on 23 April.2019).

[3] Franjo Sušac (Text und Foto), Conect Mostar (and design), *Medjugorje MONOGRAFIA PER I PELLEGRINI,* Grafotisak, Grude 2014, page 6.

[4] Ljubica Benović, *Medjugorje A Little Encyclopaedia*, Euterpa Drinovci and Pogledača, Zagreb, Drinovci 2010, page 26.

Today, the pilgrim site is looked after by Franciscan monks.[5]

During the Bosnian war, Medjugorje was under the authority of the Croatian Defence Council. In 1995, as a result of the Dayton Agreement, it became part of the Federation of Bosnia and Herzegovina. Medjugorje itself, lies in the county of Herzegovina - Neretva, which is one of 10 autonomous regions. This division into regions is to prevent that one ethnic group dominates the new Federation.

It is typical for Marian apparitions, that the visionaries will be treated with hostility by their surroundings or not be taken seriously. Such was also the case in Medjugorje. The children were immediately interrogated by the Yugoslav police and were subjected to psychiatric examinations. Yet, no health conspicuities could be established.[6] The parish priest at the time, Father Jozo Zovko, did not initially believe in the authenticity of the Marian apparitions. When, however, our Lady appeared to him while praying the rosary at St. James Church, he became an unbending advocate of the apparitions.[7] He even went to prison for three and a half years for having given a homily about the Israelites wandering through the desert for 40 years, since the Yugolasv police constructed his sermon to be a reference to the 40th anniversary of the revolution. [8] His

---

[5] Udruga Međugorje - MIR, Split, HR „ Ein kurzer historischer Überblick " in medjugorje.hr 2019, under: http://www.medjugorje.hr/de/pfarrei/geschichte/ (retrieved on: 11 April 2019).
[6] Angela Mahmoodzada u. Beatrix Zureich, *Mejugorje Kurzbericht*, 1. ed., Miriam Verlag, 79798 Jestetten, 2010, p. 27.
[7] Angela Mahmoodzada u. Beatrix Zureich, *Mejugorje Kurzbericht*, 1. ed., Miriam Verlag, 79798 Jestetten, 2010, p. 18.
[8] Sabrina Čovič – Radojičić, *Begegnungen mit Pater Jozo*, Les Editions Sakramento, 75014 Paris, Frankreich, 2014, Location 949.

lawyer, however, managed to have his sentence reduced to one and a half years.[9]

Next to our Lady, the visionaries also saw our Lord Jesus Christ. Some of them were also permitted to take a glimpse into Hell, Purgatory and Paradise. Before every apparition, the visionaries usually see a triple flash.[10] Although the "Medjugorje apparitions" can be compared to those of Fatima (Portugal), Akita (Japan) and Kibeho (Rwanda), none of them lasted as long as those of Medjugorje. According to a message to the visionary Marija, Our Lady even places the apparitions of Medjugorje in direct reference to those of Fatima. "...I invite you to self - renunciation for nine days so that, with your help, everything that I desire to realize through the secrets I began in Fatima, may be fulfilled." (message from 25 August 1991).[11]

THE CORE MESSAGE (derived from various messages)

One might think that once one has visited the holy places and is on one´s way home, one has fulfilled one´s pilgrim duty. But in my opinion, Medjugorje really takes place at home, namely through the implementation of the message.

Based on the messages, the following 5 - part message (called stones) can be identified:

[9] Sabrina Čovič – Radojičić, *Begegnungen mit Pater Jozo*, Les Editions Sakramento, 75014 Paris, France, 2014, *Location* 1129.
[10] Angela Mahmoodzada u. Beatrix Zureich, *Mdejugorje Kurzbericht*, 1. ed., Miriam Verlag, 79798 Jestetten, 2010, p. 19.
[11] Medjugorje - Apologia.com, *The Messages of Medjugorje: The Complete Text, 1981-2014*, 2014, p. 120.

- **Call to confession**

- **Call to prayer**

  - especially the daily prayer of the Holy Rosary (see prayer attachment)

- **Call to fasting**

  - every Wednesday and Friday

  - with bread and water

- **Attendance of the Holy Mass**

- **Lecture of the Holy Bible**

PROMINENT MESSAGES [12] [13]

Message from 28 October 1981: [14]

"'Where you there at Križevac yesterday for half an hour?' Yes, didn't you see me?' (DV. 1,17; CP. 251). Several hundred people saw, at the site of the first apparition, a fire which burned without burning up anything. In the evening, the Virgin tells the seers: The fire seen by the faithful was of a supernatural character. It is one of the signs; a forerunner of the great sign.' (CP. 25)"

---

[12] The italics in the original have been removed in all messages.

[13] Mistakes in spelling, punctuation and capitalisation have been corrected in all messages. For the sake of fluency, however, these corrections are not pointed out to by means of (sic!).

[14] Medjugorje - Apologia.com, *The Messages of Medjugorje: The Complete Text, 1981 - 2014*, 2014, p. 39.

Message from 21 July 1982: [15]

"There are many souls in Purgatory. There are also persons who have been consecrated to God: some priests, some religious. Pray for their intentions, at least seven Our Father´s, Hail Mary´s and Glory Be´s and the Creed. I recommend it to you. There is a large number of souls who have been in Purgatory for a long time because no one prays for them. A response to a question on fasting: The best fast is on bread and water. Through fasting and prayer, one can stop wars, one can suspend the laws of nature. Charity cannot replace fasting. Those who are not able to fast can sometimes replace it with prayer, charity and a confession; but everyone, except the sick, must fast. (CP 69)"

Message from 24 July 1982: [16]

"Answer to some questions which were asked: We go to Heaven in full conscience: that which we have now. At the moment of death, we are conscious of the separation of the body and the soul. It is false to teach people that we are re-born many times and that we pass to different bodies. One is born only once. The body, drawn from the earth, decomposes after death. It never comes back to life again. Man receives a transfigured body. Whoever has done very much evil during his life can go straight to Heaven if he confesses, is sorry for what he has done, and received Communion at the end of his life. (CP 70)".

[15] Medjugorje - Apologia.com, *The Messages of Medjugorje: The Complete Text, 1981 - 2014*, 2014, p. 49.
[16] Medjugorje - Apologia.com, *The Messages of Medjugorje: The Complete Text, 1981- 2014*, 2014, p. 49.

Message from 25 July 1982: [17]

"A response to questions which were asked concerning Hell: Today many persons go to Hell. God permits his children to suffer in Hell due to the fact that they have committed grave unpardonable sins. Those who are in Hell, no longer have a chance to know a better lot. (CP 71)

Response to questions regarding cures: for the cure of the sick, it is important to say the following prayers: the Creed, seven Our Father´s, Hail Mary´s and Glory Be´s and to fast on bread and water. It is good to impose (sic!) one´s hands on the sick and pray. It is good to anoint the sick with holy oil. All priests do not have the gift of healing. In order to revive this gift, the priest must pray with perseverance and believe firmly. (CP 71)."

Message from 6 August 1982: [18]

"A response to questions which were asked concerning confession. One must invite people to go to confession each month, especially the first SATURDAY. Here I have not spoken about it yet. I have invited people to frequent confession, I will give you yet some concrete messages for our time. Be patient because the time has not yet come. Do what I have told you. There are numerous who do not observe it. Monthly confession will be a remedy for the Church in the West. One must convey this message to the West. (CP 72)."

---

[17] Medjugorje - Apologia.com, *The Messages of Medjugorje: The Complete Text, 1981 - 2014*, 2014, page 49.
[18] Medjugorje - Apologia.com, *The Messages of Medjugorje: The Complete Text, 1981 - 2014*, 2014, pages 49 - 50.

Message from 8 January 1984: [19]

"My children, pray! I say it again, pray! I will say it to you again. Do not think that Jesus is going to manifest Himself again in the manger: Friends, He is born again in your hearts. (DN 1,30)."

Message from early 1984: [20]

"…When you are in the room of the apparitions or at the church, you should not preoccupy yourself with taking pictures. You should rather use the time to pray to Jesus, especially in those moments of particular grace during the apparitions. (T.58)."

Message from 19 April 1984: [21]

"Message for the parish! Dear children, share my compassion: pray, pray, pray! To Jelena: I´m going to reveal a spiritual secret to you: If you want to be stronger than evil, make yourself a plan of personal prayer. Take a certain time in the morning, read a text from Holy Scripture, anchor the Divine word in your heart, and strive to live if during the day, particularly during the moment of trials. In this way, you will be stronger than evil. (Bl. 186). That same day, the Blessed Virgin had `dictated´ to Jelena the following prayer: HOW TO GIVE ONESELF TO MARY, MOTHER OF GOODNESS, OF LOVE AND OF MERCY.

---

[19] Medjugorje - Apologia.com, *The Messages of Medjugorje: The Complete Text, 1981 - 2014*, 2014, page 65.

[20] Medjugorje - Apologia.com, *The Messages of Medjugorje: The Complete Text, 1981 - 2014*, 2014, pp. 64, 65.

[21] Medjugorje - Apologia.com, *The Messages of Medjugorje: The Complete Text, 1981 - 2014*, 2014, pp. 70, 71.

"Oh my Mother! Mother of Goodness, love and mercy! I love you immensely, and I offer myself to you. Through your goodness, your love, and your mercy, save me! I wish to be yours. I love you immensely and I wish that you protect me. In my heart, oh Mother of Goodness give me your goodness. So that I go to Heaven. I ask you for your immense love that you may give me the grace. That I will be able to love each one just like you loved Jesus Christ. I ask you in grace that I be able to be merciful ı to you. I offer myself completely to you and I wish that you will be with me at each step, because you are full of grace, and if I should lose it, I will ask, make me find it again. Amen. ….."

ı According to Fr. Slavko, it means: `That I know how to love your will when it differs from mine.´"

Message from 14 August 1984: [22]

"I ask the people to pray with me these days, as much as they can. Fast strictly on WEDNESDAYS and FRIDAYS. Every day at least one rosary, Joyful, Sorrowful and Glorious mysteries. (C.150)."

Message from October 1984: [23]

"…When you go to mass, your trip from home to church should be a time of preparation for mass. You should also receive Holy Communion with an open and pure heart; purity of heart and openness. Do not leave the church without an appropriate act of thanksgiving. I can help you only if you are accessible to my suggestions; I can not (sic!) help you if you are not open. (T-59). The most important in

[22] Medjugorje - Apologia.com, *The Messages of Medjugorje: The Complete Text, 1981 - 2014*, 2014, page 76.
[23] Medjugorje - Apologia.com, *The Messages of Medjugorje: The Complete Text, 1981 - 2014*, 2014, page 78.

spiritual life is to ask for the gift of the Holy Spirit. When
the Holy Spirit comes, then peace will be established. When
that occurs, everything changes around you. Things will
change (T.59)."

Message from 1984 - 1985: [24]

"On the matter of a Catholic priest, confused because of the
cure of an Orthodox child: Tell this priest, tell everyone,
that it is you who is divided on earth. The Muslims and the
Orthodox, for the same reason as Catholics, are equal before
my Son and me. You are all my children. Certainly, all
religions are not equal, but all men are equal before God, as
St. Paul says. It does not suffice to belong to the Catholic
Church to be saved, but it is necessary to respect the
commandments of God in following one´s conscience.
Those who are not Catholics, are no less creatures made in
the image of God, and destined to rejoin someday, the
House of the Father, Salvation is available to everyone,
without exception. Only those who refuse God deliberately,
are condemned. To him, who has been given little, little will
be asked for. To whomever has been given much (to
Catholics), very much will be required. It is God alone, in
His infinite justice, Who determines the degree of
responsibility and pronounces judgment. (C128)."

Message from 22 August 1985: [25]

"Dear children! Today I wish to tell you that the Lord wants
to put you to the test, which you can overcome by prayer.
God puts you to the test in your daily activities. Pray now

---

[24] Medjugorje - Apologia.com, *The Messages of Medjugorje: The Complete
Text, 1981 - 2014*, 2014, page 104.
[25] Medjugorje - Apologia.com, *The Messages of Medjugorje: The Complete
Text, 1981 - 2014*, 2014, pp. 87, 88.

that you pass every test peacefully. Come through every test from God more open to HIM and approach Him with greater love."

Message from 25 October 1988: [26]

"Dear children! My invitation that you live the messages which I am giving you is a daily one, specially, because I want to draw you closer to the Heart of Jesus. Therefore, little children, I am inviting you today to the prayer of consecration to Jesus, my dear Son, so that each of you may be His. And then I am inviting you to the consecration of my Immaculate Heart. I want you to consecrate yourselves as parents, as families and as parishioners so that all belong to God through my heart. Therefore, little children, pray that you comprehend the greatness of this message which I am giving you. I do not want anything for myself, rather all for the salvation of your soul. Satan is strong and therefore, you, little children, by constant prayer, press tightly against my motherly heart. Thank you for having responded to my call." (for the prayer of consecration; see appendix)

Message from 25 July 1991: [27]

"Dear children! Today I invite you to pray for peace. At this time peace is being threatened in a special way, and I am seeking from you to renew fasting and prayer in your families. I desire you to grasp the seriousness of the situation and that much of what will happen depends on your prayers and you are praying a little bit…"

---

[26] Medjugorje - Apologia.com, *The Messages of Medjugorje: The Complete Text, 1981 - 2014*, 2014, page 117.
[27] Medjugorje - Apologia.com, *The Messages of Medjugorje: The Complete Text, 1981 - 2014*, 2014, page 120.

Message from 25 November 1998: [28]

"…The holy confession shall be your first step towards
conversion."

Message from 25 February 2003: [29]

"Dear children. Today, also, I call you to pray and fast for
peace. As I have already said and now repeat to you, little
children, through prayer and fasting wars can be stopped, as
well. Peace is a precious gift of God. Seek, ask and you
shall receive him. Speak of peace and carry the peace in
your hearts. Nurture him like a flower that needs water,
sensitivity and light. Be the ones who bring peace to the
others. I am with you and intercede for all of you all. Thank
you for having answered to my call."

Message from 25 October 2008: [30]

"Dear children! In a special way I call you all to pray for my
intentions so that, through your prayers, you may stop
Satan´s plan over this world, which is further from God
every day, and which puts itself in the place of God and is
destroying everything that is beautiful and good in the souls
of each of you. Therefore, little children, arm yourselves
with prayer and fasting so that you may be conscious of
how much God loves you and may carry out God´s will.
Thank you for having responded to my call."

---

[28] Angela Mahmoodzada u. Beatrix Zureich, *Medjugorje Kurzbericht*, 1. Aufl.,
Miriam Verlag, 79798 Jestetten, 2010, page 38 (translation into English: the
author).
[29] Medjugorje - Apologia.com, *The Messages of Medjugorje: The Complete
Text, 1981 - 2014*, 2014, page 132.
[30] Medjugorje - Apologia.com, *The Messages of Medjugorje: The Complete
Text, 1981 - 2014*, 2014, page 136.

Message from 2 April 2015: [31]

"Dear children! My apostles, I have chosen you because all
of you carry something beautiful within you. You can help
me, so that the love, for which my Son died and then rose
again, will be victorious once again. My apostles, that is
why I am calling you to try to see something good in every
creature of God, in all my children, and to try to understand
them. My children, you are all brothers and sisters through
the same Holy Spirit. You, who are filled with love for my
Son, can tell what you know to all those who have not
gotten to know this love. You have come to know the love
of my Son, you have understood His Resurrection, with joy
you raise your eyes to Him. It is my motherly wish, that all
of my children are united in the love for Jesus. My apostles,
that is why I call you to live the Eucharist with joy, because
in the Eucharist my Son always gives himself to you anew
and through His example, He shows the love and sacrifice
for the neighbour. I thank you!"

Message from 2 January 2019: [32]

"Dear children. Unfortunately, there are, among you, my
children, so many fights, hatred, personal interests,
selfishness. My children, you so easily forget my Son, His
words, His love. In many souls, faith is being extinguished
and hearts are seized by material things of the world. But
my motherly heart knows that there are still those who
believe and love, who seek how they can come even closer
to my Son, who tirelessly seek my Son - in this way they
also seek me. Those are the humble and the meek ones, with

---

[31] Mario Vasilj, *Medjugorje Aposteln der Gospa Mirjana bezeugt*, Ogranak
Matice hrvatske u Čitluk 2015, book cover. (translation: the author).
[32] Gebetsaktion Medjugorje Wien: *„Botschaften an Mirjana"* in
www.gebetsaktion.at, under:
http://www.gebetsaktion.at/medjugorje-botschaften/botschaften-an-mirjana/
(retrieved on 14 April 2019). (translation into English: the author).

their pain and suffering, which they carry in silence, with their hopes and above all with their faith. Those are the apostles of my love.

My children, apostles of my love, I teach you that my Son does not only ask for constant prayers, but also for works and feelings, that you believe, that you pray, that you grow through personal prayers in the faith, that you grow in love. To love one another, that is what He is seeking, that is the way to eternal life. My children do not forget that my Son has brought the light into this world, and He brought it to those who wanted to see and receive it. You, be the ones, as this is the light of the truth, of peace and of love.

I guide you motherly, so that you may adore my Son, that you love my Son together with me, that your thoughts, words and works may be directed towards my Son, that they be in His name. Then my heart will be filled. I thank you."

Message from 2 September 2019: [33]

"Dear children! Pray the rosary every day – this wreath of flowers, which connects me, as a mother, directly with your pain, suffering, wishes and hopes. Apostles of my love, I am with you, through the grace and the love of my Son, and I request prayers from you. The world is in such need of your prayers, so that the souls may be converted. Open your hearts to my Son with complete trust and He will inscribe in them the summary of his Word - and that is love. Live in unbreakable union with the most sacred heart of my Son. My children, as a mother, I tell you that it is high time to kneel down before my Son, to confess Him as your God - the centre of your life. Offer Him the gifts, which He loves the most, and that is love for your neighbour, mercy and

---

[33] Medjugorje Web Site, *„BOTSCHAFTEN VON MEDJUGORJE"* in www.medjugorje.ws under: https://www.medjugorje.ws/de/messages/ (retrieved on 19 September 2019).

pure hearts. Apostles of my love, many of my children do not acknowledge my Son as their God yet, they haven´t experienced His love. You, on the other hand, will, through your prayer, which is said from a pure and open heart, together with the offerings you will bring to my Son, cause that even the hardest of hearts will be opened. Apostles of my love, the power of prayer which is said from the heart - powerful prayers full of love - change the world. Hence, my children, pray, pray, pray. I am with you.“

Message from 25 January 1987: [34]

“Today, I want to appeal to all of you to start living a new life from this day on. Dear children, I wished that you would understand that God has chosen each one of you to have a part in the great plan for the salvation of mankind. You cannot fully understand how great your role is in God´s design. For that reason, pray, dear children, so that through prayer, you may be able to know your role in God´s plan. I am with you, so that you may be able to realise it fully.”

Annotation: All published messages can be viewed, inter alia, at the following websites:
/http://www.medjugorje.eu/messages [35],

---

[34] Medjugorje - Apologia.com, *The Messages of Medjugorje: The Complete Text, 1981 - 2014*, 2014, pp. 97,98.
[35] The Riehle Foundation, *„All 1300 messages from the beginning until today on one page”* in MESSAGES AND TEACHINGS OF MARY AT MEDJUGORJE under: http://www.medjugorje.eu/messages/ (retrieved on 6 April 2020).

www.medjugorje.ws [36] and www.medjugorje.de [37] (this information is provided without warranty)

THE TEN SECRETS

Part of the messages are also ten secrets.

When it comes to the secrets, Mirjana Soldo plays a prominent role. She, inter alia, received all 10 secrets on 25 December 1982, in form of a scroll. Mirjana showed this scroll to a female or male cousin and a friend (more details are not known), but no one, except Mirjana, could perceive the content in its actual form. The others saw something like a prayer or a request for help.[38]

The Blessed Mother asked Mirjana to choose a priest of her trust. Ten days before the occurrence of the first secret, she shall entrust the secret to him. Mirjana chose Father Petar Ljubičić. Both shall fast and pray for 7 days, before revealing the secret.

The first two secrets concern warnings to the world. These events will happen during Mirjana´s lifetime. Also, the messages of Medjugorje, are to be subsequently legitimised

---

[36] Medjugorje Web Site, „*BOTSCHAFTEN VON MEDJUGORJE*" in www.medjugorje.ws unter: https://www.medjugorje.ws/de/messages/ (retrieved on 12 July 2019).

[37] Deutschsprachiges Informationszentrum für Medjugorje, „*Alle bisherigen Botschaften der Muttergottes*" *in* medjugorje wo der Himmel die Erde berührt unter: https://www.medjugorje.de/botschaften/alle-botschaften/ (retrieved on 12 July 2019).

[38] Lynch, Dan, *The Ten Secrets of the blessed Virgin Mary*, John Paul Press, St. Albans, VT 05478, USA, 2011, pp. 20, 22.

through the occurrence of the two secrets.[39] To be more exact, the first secret refers to a great unrest in the world.[40]

The second secret refers to the illumination of conscience. This is understood to be a small day of judgement.[41]

The third secret announces the appearance of a visible and permanent sign on Apparition Hill.[42] Parallel to the appearance of the sign, there will be miracles and healings.[43]

Nothing is known about the 4th, 5th and 6th secret.[44]

After the appearance of the visible sign, man can convert for a short period of time. Then, however, the chastisements will follow. The punishments are predicted in secrets 7 - 10.[45]

---

[39] Lynch, Dan, *The Ten Secrets of the blessed Virgin Mary*, John Paul Press, St. Albans, VT 05478, USA, 2011, p. 23.

[40] prolifeformankind.com „*The 10 Secrets of Medjugorje: "What you need to know"* " in YOU TUBE pblished on: 14. April 2014 (retrieved on 14 April 2019).

[41] prolifeformankind.com: „*The 10 Secrets of Medjugorje: "What you need to know"* " in YOU TUBE, published on: 14. April 2014 (retrieved on 14 April 2019).

[42] www.saturdaynightspirit.com: „*Die Erscheinungen von Medjugorje (seit 1981)* "
in Saturday Night Spirit, under:
https://www.saturdaynightspirit.com/medjugorje/ (retrieved on 14. April 2019).

[43] www.saturdaynightspirit.com: „*Die Erscheinungen von Medjugorje (seit 1981)* "
In Saturday Night Spirit, under:
https://www.saturdaynightspirit.com/medjugorje/ (retrieved on 14 April 2019).

[44] prolifeformankind.com: „*The 10 Secrets of Medjugorje: 'What you need to know*" in YOU TUBE, published on: 14. April 2014 (retrieved on 14 April 2019).

[45] Lynch, Dan, *The Ten Secrets of the blessed Virgin Mary*, John Paul Press, St. Albans, VT 05478, USA, 2011, p. 21.

According to Mirjana, the chastisement which is predicted in the 7th secret, can be moderated through prayer. [46] [47]

The penalisation, which is proclaimed in the 8th secret, frightened Mirjana to such an extent, that she asked for mercy for humanity. The punishment was mitigated, but cannot, however, be avoided completely.[48]

The impending calamity, which is predicted in the 9th secret, can still be mitigated by prayer.[49]

The punishment of the 10th secret, contains, amongst other things, 3 days of darkness and cannot be moderated by prayer.[50] The punishment is caused by fact, that not all people will be converted.[51]

Message pertaining to the warnings (25. August 1997): [52]

"Dear children! God grants me this time as a gift for you, in order to teach you how to get to the path of salvation and can lead you to it. Dear children, now you don´t understand

---

[46] You Tube: The 10 Secrets of Medjugorje: "What you need to know" by prolifeformankind.com, published on 14 April 2014 (retrieved on 14 April 2019).

[47] The Ten Secrets of the Blessed Virgin Mary by Dan Lynch, p. 26.

[48] Medjugorje - Apologia.com, *The Messages of Medjugorje: The Complete Text, 1981 - 2014*, 2014, page 51, message from 6. November 1982.

[49] Lynch, Dan, *The Ten Secrets of the blessed Virgin Mary*, John Paul Press, St. Albans, VT 05478, USA, 2011, p. 26.

[50] Lynch, Dan, *The Ten Secrets of the blessed Virgin Mary*, John Paul Press, St. Albans, VT 05478, USA, 2011, p. 26 and

You Tube: The 10 Secrets of Medjugorje: "What you need to know" by prolifeformankind.com, (based on the book„The Last Apparition" by Wayne Weible 3. January 2013), published on 14 April 2014 (retrieved on 14 April 2019).

[51] You Tube: The 10 Secrets of Medjugorje: "What you need to know" by prolifeformankind.com, published on 14. April 2014 (retrieved on 14 April 2019).

[52] Medjugorje - Apologia.com, *The Messages of Medjugorje: The Complete Text, 1981 - 2014*, 2014, page 126.

this blessing, but there will soon come a time when you will lament for these messages."

Mirjana's view of the punishments: "I would like to suggest to you, that you do not talk about the punishments, since Our Lady came to Medjugorje in order to help us and not to destroy us. She said,

`*What I began in Fatima, I will finish in Medjugorje. My heart will triumph.*´

If the heart of Our Divine Mother will triumph, then what is there to fear?" [53]

PILGRIM STATIONS IN MEDJUGORJE

1.   Apparition Hill (Podbrdo)
and Blue Cross

Apparition Hill is the first place, where Our Lady appeared to the visionaries for the first time. A steadily ascending, rough, stony path leads up the Hill. The climb takes about half an hour. The path is lined with bronze reliefs by the Italian sculptor Prof. Carmelo Puzzolo.[54] The reliefs depict the Mysteries of the Joyful and the Sorrowful Rosary. They were set up in 1989. At the top, you will find a large statue of Our Lady. It is a replica of the statue of Mary created by Dino Felici, which is located on the forecourt of the parish church. The replica was donated by South Korean pilgrims

---

[53] Lynch, Dan, *The Ten Secrets of the blessed Virgin Mary*, John Paul Press, St. Albans, VT 05478, USA, 2011, p. 27.

[54] Carmelo Puzzolo was once a pilgrim in Medjugorje himself. The idea to sculpt the bronze reliefs was born after a spontaneous meeting with Father Slavko Barbarić.
Source: Medjugorje Deutschland e.V.: *„Entstehung der Bronzetafeln auf den Bergen"* in: medjugorje Wo der Himmel die Erde berührt (Source reference: Magazine Oase des Friedens 10/2014) (retrieved on 17 July 2019).

in gratitude for the healing of their son. [55] The statue was inaugurated by Father Ivan Sesar.[56] There is also a large wooden Tyrolean cross on Apparition Hill, which was donated by pilgrims from Bolzano.[57]

There are three "entrances" from where you can start your climb up Podbrdo. The first entry, coming from the village on Kraljice Mira, is at Kraljice Mira 43. If this is your starting point, the "walk" is approximately 5 - 10 minutes longer than if one takes off at the other two entrances. But this path is an easier "climb". At the beginning of the path there is a large wooden cross on the right. It marks the place where the Blessed Mother asked for peace for the first time.[58]

The other two entrances can be reached by keeping on walking on Kraljice Mira for about 80 metres. The entrances are then on the left and right hand of a church. These entrances lead also to the so - called **Blue Cross**. This is a prayer station which is at the beginning of the ascent. The location is named after several large blue crosses, which were erected there together with statues of the Virgin Mary. Pilgrims who cannot climb the entire hill, can pray here. Those who want to pray the entire Rosary while climbing up and down Apparition Hill, should start at entrances 2 or 3 and then follow the reliefs. The tour then ends at "Entrance 1". It is good to know that there is the possibility to be carried upon Apparition Hill on a stretcher. To organise an ascent on a stretcher, I would contact the Information Centre.

---

[55] Ljubica Benović, *Medjugorje A Little* Encyclopaedia, Publishers: Euterpa Drinovci and Pogledača, Zagreb, Drinovci 2010, page 42.
[56] Franjo Sušac (Text und Foto), Conect Mostar (und Design), Medjugorje *MONOGRAFIA PER I PELLEGRINI,* Grafotisak, Grude 2014, page 18.
[57] Franjo Sušac (Text und Foto), Conect Mostar (und Design), Medjugorje *MONOGRAFIA PER I PELLEGRINI,* Grafotisak, Grude 2014, page 16.
[58] Ljubica Benović, *Medjugorje A Little Encyclopaedia*, Publishers: Euterpa Drinovci and Pogledača, Zagreb, Drinovci 2010, page 42.

The paths to Apparition Hill are illuminated at night.

Frequently Marian apparitions also take place at the Blue Cross.

Unfortunately, there has been a change to this subject since 18 March 2020. Until 2 March 2020, the visionary Mirjana received a message here every 2nd of the month. In her birthday message on 18 March 2020, Our Lady told Mirjana that this is now over. Mirjana will now only receive a message on her birthday, the 18th March. [59]

Since I assume that these messages will continue to take place in public and at the Blue Cross, I leave the subsequent text. It describes how the apparitions at the Blue Cross have taken place in the past.

At the time of a Marian apparition, a path for the seer is fenced off at the 3rd entrance. (Personal note: Unfortunately, many pilgrims do not keep a minimal, appropriate distance to Mirjana) Some pilgrims even spend the whole night at the Blue Cross to be right next to Mirjana during the apparition. Even if you don´t camp the entire night at the Blue Cross, you should be there by 7.00 am, at the latest. From 8.00 a.m. onwards, the Rosary is prayed and is usually followed by the apparition. The apparition is generally preceded by prayer and singing. The vision lasts about 10 minutes. Since many pilgrims come from Italy, the Rosary and the songs are mostly in Italian. That the Blessed

---

[59] Stephen Ryan:„ *Visionary Mirjana's apparitions with the Blessed Mother on the 2nd of the month have permanently ended. Will appear to Mirjana once a year on her birthday.*", in MYSTIC POST 18. März 2020, under: https://mysticpost.com/2020/03/visionary-mirjanas-apparitions-with-the-blessed-mother-on-the-2nd-of-the-month-has-permanently-ended-will-appear-to-mirjana-once-a-year-on-her-birthday/ (retrieved on 2 April 2020).

Mother appears, can only be known by the sudden silence or by the loudly proclaimed word: "Silenzio!" (Silence!).

A large gravel parking lot is located near the 3rd entrance. Buses and regular cars cab park here. If you want to park here, at the time of a Marian apparition, you should be early.

Annotation to public Marian Apparitions:

- The Seer Marija continues to have visions of Our Lady on every 25th of the month. These visions are somewhat public. They usually take place at her own hotel complex, the „Magnificat". (see POSSIBLE CONTACT TO THE VISIONARIES, page 60).

- Sometimes the visionary Ivan also has spontaneous apparitions of Our Lady at the Blue Cross. Therefore, it is advisable to check daily at your place of residence whether something special is taking place.

● … My eyes and my heart will be here, even when I will no longer appear… (excerpt from the message to Mirjana on 18. March 1996) [60] ●

---

[60] *Medjugorje 1981 – 2019: History of the apparitions and the messages of the Queen of Peace from 1981 to 2018*, Matica Hrvatska Čitluc, 2019, page 165.

Statue of Our Lady on Podbrodo

Tirolean Cross on Apparition Hill

Relief on Apparition Hill

Blue Cross

Path on Apparition Hill

Here Our Lady asked for peace for the first time

2.   St. James Church

The construction of the parish church took 34 years, from 1935 until 1969.[61] Mother Mary appeared to the visionary - children several times at the church.[62]

The "Queen of Peace" Statue, created by Dino Felici, is situated in the square in front of the church. It was erected in 1987.[63] In the vicinity of the statue are two fountains. In winter, however, the fountains are turned off. But not to worry, according to the analysis of a research team from Milan, Italy, with Mrs. Gigi Capriolo presiding, every water which is brought from Medjugorje takes on the vibrations of the "fountain" water. According to the analysis, the water from Medjugorje is said to be uplifting and mesodermic. Hence, it is said to have positive effects on the spine, muscles and joints. It also claimed to aid with the regulation of the nervous system.[64]

---

[61] Ljubica Benović, *Medjugorje A Little Encyclopaedia*, Publishers: Euterpa Drinovci and Pogledača, Zagreb, Drinovci 2010, page 33.
[62] Sabrina Čovič – Radojičić, *Begegnungen mit Pater Jozo*, Les Editions Sakramento, 75014 Paris, France, 2014, *Location* 807.
[63] Ljubica Benović, *Medjugorje A Little Encyclopaedia*, Publishers: Euterpa Drinovci and Pogledača, Zagreb, Drinovci 2010, page 52.
[64] Father Bernward Maria Weiss, „*Die Wunderwasser heiliger Orte*"
in www.kath-zdw.ch under: http://kath-zdw.ch/maria/wallfahrtsorte.wundertaetiges.wasser.html (retrieved on 18 April 2019).

St. James Church from within

St. James Church side view

"Queen of Peace" Statue in the square of St. James Church

Statue of the Gospa in St. James Church

Con-fessionals next to St. James Church

3.   Križevac - Cross Mountain [65] [66]

The Cross Mountain is the "mountain" above Medjugorje, upon which a 8.56 m high concrete cross was erected by the parish members in 1934.[67] The inscription reads: "IHS Jesus, Christ the Redeemer of the human race as a sign of his faith, his love and his hope erected by P. Bernardin Smoljan priest and by the parish of Medjugorje. Deliver us from all evil O Jesus!" [68]

Relics were placed at the intersection of the cross. The relics were donated by Rome. Since the erection of the cross, Holy Mass is celebrated on the Mountain on the Feast of the Exaltation of the Cross (1st Sunday after Mary's birth). With the onset of the apparitions of Our Lady, the faithful began to pray the Way of the Cross on Cross Mountain.

I would like to mention that after one Marian apparition, the golden, handwritten word PEACE was often seen by pilgrims in the sky above Križevac. Our Lady also proclaimed on Cross Mountain that she is the 'Queen of Peace'. [69] The visionaries state that Our Lady commented on Cross (Mountain), on 30. August 1984 in the following way: [70]

„Dear children, the Cross was part of the plan when you erected it. Let everyone go, on his own, on the mountain and

---

[65] The italics in the original have been removed in all messages.

[66] Mistakes in spelling, punctuation and capitalisation have been corrected in all messages. For the sake of fluency, however, these corrections are not pointed out to by means of (sic!).

[67] Angela Mahmoodzada u. Beatrix Zureich, *Medjugorje Kurzbericht*, 1. Aufl., Miriam Verlag, 79798 Jestetten, 2010, page 36.

[68] Mario Vasilj, *Medjugorje Aposteln der Gospa Mirjana bezeugt*, Ogranak Matice hrvatske u Čitluk 2015, page 137.

[69] Angela Mahmoodzada u. Beatrix Zureich, *Medjugorje Kurzbericht*, 1. Aufl., Miriam Verlag, 79798 Jestetten, 2010, page 36.

[70] Mario Vasilj, *Medjugorje Aposteln der Gospa Mirjana bezeugt*, Ogranak Matice hrvatske u Čitluk 2015, page 96.

pray underneath the Cross. I need your prayers. Thank you for having answered my call!"

On 24 November 2000 a bronze relief, in honour of Pater Slavko Barbarić was erected. Pater Barbarić had rendered great service to Medjugorje. He had died one year prior at the site of the relief as a result of a heart attack. At the time of his death, he was accompanied by a group of pilgrims.[71]

The entrance to Cross Mountain is located at the Put Križevaca. Opposite the `entrance´ is a small parking lot. Despite of the parking meter, parking is free of charge.

The path is as rocky and steep as the one to Podbrdo. But one should allow up to 1 hour 15 minutes for the ascent.

If one also prays the Way of the Cross, the ascent takes about 1 hour 30 minutes. The path is also lined with bronze reliefs, this time to pray the Stations of the Cross.

The path to Križevac is not illuminated at night.

If you experience problems on the ascend or descend: The first aid number is: 0038736650201

---

[71] Angela Mahmoodzada u. Beatrix Zureich, *Medjugorje Kurzbericht*, 1. Aufl., Miriam Verlag, 79798 Jestetten, 2010, page 36.

Križevac Cross

Path to Cross Mountain

Relief of Pater Slavko Barbarić

4.   The Via Domini

The avenue that bears the name Via Domini (the way of the Lord) is located behind St. James Church. It leads towards Križevac.

Along this avenue, 5 mosaics are erected, representing the Luminous Mysteries of the Rosary.[72]

One should not be surprised to find horses being "parked" here during the night.

---

[72] Travel-medjugorje.com:„*The top 10 things to do while in Medjugorje*", in whl.travel 2016, under:
https://www.travel-medjugorje.com/travel-info/The-top-10-things-to-do-while-in-medjugorje (retrieved on 14 April 2019).

5. The Statue of the Risen Christ

Once one has passed all 5 mosaics on the Via Domini,
coming from St. James Church, the Statue of the Risen
Christ is on the right - hand side. The Slovenian sculptor
Andrej Ajdič donated the Statue to the parish on the first
day of Easter.[73]

Astonishingly, the Statue has been secreting a fluid from
underneath the right knee since the year 2000. [74]

Various physicists have examined the Statue, but couldn´t
come up with a logical explanation for the phenomenon.[75]
The Italian expert of "the Shroud of Turin", Professor
Giulio Fanti, from the University of Padua, has analysed the
liquid and came to the following finding: The liquid
consists of 99% water, but also contains traces of calcium,
copper, iron, potassium, magnesium, sodium, sulphur and

---

[73] Stephen Ryan*: „ Medjugorje. The unveiled mysteries of the statue of the risen
Christ. “*, in MYSTIC POST 9. August 2018, under:
https://mysticpost.com/2018/08/medjugorje-the-unveiled-mysteries-of-the-
statue-of-the-risen-christ/ (retrieved on 11. April 2019).
[74] Medjugorje Web Online Store: „*Risen Christ*" under:
https://medjugorje.org/ccart/statues/risen-christ.html (retrieved on 21 April
2019).
[75] Medjugorje Web Online Store: „*Risen Christ*" under:
https://medjugorje.org/ccart/statues/risen-christ.html (retrieved on 21 April
2019).

zinc.[76] The liquid also crystallises in the dried state.[77] Many pilgrims wipe the droplets, which are said to have healing properties, off the Statue and bring them to the sick.[78]

The hip area of the Statue was covered by the artist with newspaper on which Psalm 138 is written.[79]

Please be prepared to wait patiently in line until you reach the Statue. The wait can sometimes take up to half an hour.

The little square, in which the Statue is situated, serves for silent prayer. Since 2002, you can also pray the Stations of the Cross here.[80] Thus pilgrims, who cannot climb up Križevac Mountain, can pray the Way of the Cross here.[81]

---

[76] Stephen Ryan: „*Medjugorje. The unveiled mysteries of the statue of the risen Christ.*", in MYSTIC POST 9 August 2018, under:
https://mysticpost.com/2018/08/medjugorje-the-unveiled-mysteries-of-the-statue-of-the-risen-christ/ (retrieved on 11 April 2019).

[77] Stephen Ryan: „*Medjugorje. The unveiled mysteries of the statue of the risen Christ.*", in MYSTIC POST 9 August 2018, under:
https://mysticpost.com/2018/08/medjugorje-the-unveiled-mysteries-of-the-statue-of-the-risen-christ/ (retrieved on 11 April 2019).

[78] Stephen Ryan: „*Medjugorje. The unveiled mysteries of the statue of the risen Christ.*", in MYSTIC POST 9 August 2018, under:
https://mysticpost.com/2018/08/medjugorje-the-unveiled-mysteries-of-the-statue-of-the-risen-christ/ (retrieved on 11 April 2019).

[79] Stephen Ryan: „*Medjugorje. The unveiled mysteries of the statue of the risen Christ.*", in MYSTIC POST 9 August 2018, under:
https://mysticpost.com/2018/08/medjugorje-the-unveiled-mysteries-of-the-statue-of-the-risen-christ/ (retrieved on 11 April 2019).

[80] Medjugorje Deutschland e.V.: „*Auferstandener Jesus*", in: Medjugorje Wo der Himmel die Erde berührt, under:
https://www.medjugorje.de/medjugorje/ueber-medjugorje/orte-des-gebetes/auferstandener-jesus/ (retrieved on 21 April.2019).

[81] Travel-medjugorje.com: „*The top 10 things to do while in Medjugorje*", in whl.travel 2016, under:
https://www.travel-medjugorje.com/travel-info/The-top-10-things-to-do-while-in-medjugorje (retrieved on 14 April 2019).

6. The House of the Unborn Life

If one keeps on walking on Via Domini, after the Statue of the Risen Christ towards the cemetery, one reaches a Picture Wall of Medjugorje on the left - hand side. After the picture wall, you will find the House of the Unborn Life.

There, one has the possibility to pray for the unborn life. Multilingual literature on the topics, origin of life and abortion can also be found here.

7.   Kovačica Cemetery

At the end of Via Domini, the Kovačica Cemetery is situated. Father Slavko Barbarič is buried in here. Many pilgrims visit his grave to seek his intercession. The pilgrims lean on the message of Our Lady from 25 November 2000, in which she said: " ' *I rejoice with you and I desire to tell you that your brother Slavko has been born into Heaven and intercedes for you…' "*.[82]

---

[82] Travel-medjugorje.com:„ *The top 10 things to do while in Medjugorje* ", in whl.travel 2016, under: https://www.travel-medjugorje.com/travel-info/The-top-10-things-to-do-while-in-medjugorje (retrieved on 14 April 2019).

8.   Adoration Chapel

The Adoration Chapel is next to St. James Church. According to the prayer programme of the Information Centre, it is accessible in the afternoon. Unfortunately, I cannot confirm that this is generally true. However, the chapel is often open for church services of different pilgrim groups.

9.   Candle Park

Standing in front of St. James Church, the confessionals are on both sides of the Church. On the right - hand side, there is a doorway to the Candle Park. You can also get to the Candle Park by walking around the confessionals from the outside. Inside the Candle Park, there is a big wooden cross. This area serves the silent prayer. Here, the pilgrims can also light their votive candles.[83]

It is advantageous to carry one´s own lighter.

10.   (Social) Institutions

In the centre of Medjugorje, there are various social institutions. They were founded on the initiative of *Fr. Slavko Barbarić*. Among those institutions are two drug centres: The Village "**Cenacolo**" (ital. for cenacle)[84] and the "**Campo della Vita**" (place of life). Another institution is the "**Majčino Selo**" (Mother´s Village).[85] It was instituted after the war, which ravaged the region from 1991 – 1995.

---

[83] Travel-medjugorje.com: „*The top 10 things to do while in Medjugorje*", in whl.travel 2016, under:
https://www.travel-medjugorje.com/travel-info/The-top-10-things-to-do-while-in-medjugorje (retrieved on 14. April 2019).
[84] The Cenacolo: Kraljice Mira 108, Tel: +387 366 517 56
E-Mail: campo.della.vita@tel.net.ba, Associazione San Lorenzo – ONLUS, *Communità Cenacolo*, under:
http://www.comunitacenacolo.it/official/index.php?option=com_content&view=article&id=173 (retrieved on 23 April 2019).
[85] Tel.: +387-36-653-000
Fax +387-36-653-020
E-mail: info@mothersvillage.org
Web: www.mothersvillage.org (retrieved on 4 May 2019).

At first, it provided protection for children, who were either orphaned or abandoned, as well as for children who came from broken homes. Also children, which lived in great poverty, found refuge here. Today the social commitments of the village comprise other areas, as well.[86]

The fruit of a Scottish pilgrimage is the relief action **Mary´s Meals**.[87] The Mary's Meals "shop" is located on the Pape Ivana Paula II, in front of St. James´ Church, on the right - hand side.

The Association of the Missionary Sisters of the Wounded Family, inter alia, takes care of orphaned children and elderly people.[88]

---

[86] Hubert Liebherr: „*Medjugorje Wo der Himmel die Erde berührt*", in Medjugorje.de ‚under:
https://www.medjugorje.de/medjugorje/humanitaer/mutterdorf/ (retrieved on 4 May 2019).
[87] https://www.marysmeals.de/ (retrieved on 4 May 2019).

Mary´s Meals Deutschland e.V.
Fürstenbergerhofstr. 21
5516 Mainz
Tel.: 061312754300
E-Mail: info@marysmeals.de (the information is derived from the information brochure)

[88] Donations:
Dom za stare i iznemogle osobe "IVAN PAVAO II"
Kontonummer: 3381202253488977
IBAN: BA 393381204853587460 - EUR
SWIFT CODE: UNCRBA22
Source:
Sestre Misionarke Ranjene Obitelji: „*Contact Information*" in: Obiteljski Obiteljski Centar Papa Ivan Pauao II 2017 under:
http://www.sestre-mro.info/it/charitable-work (retrieved on 17 July 2019).

Cenacolo

Entrance to Mother´s Village

Mary´s Meals

11.   The Garden of St. Francis

It is the last project of the deceased Fr. *Slavko Barbarić*.
This garden is situated next to the Mother´s Village and
serves not only for prayer and recreation, but was also used
as a didactic institution for children. Thus, hypotherapy
(therapeutic horse - riding), e.g., was also offered here for
disabled children.[89] Unfortunately, the park has been closed
for the most part, probably for financial reasons. Only the
amphitheatre, which is well suited for Holy Masses in the
outdoors, is accessible through an entrance from within the
Mother´s Village.

---

[89] Udruga Međugorje - MIR, Split, HR „*FÜHRER DURCH DAS
HEILIGTUM DER KÖNIGIN DES FRIEDENS*" in medjugorje.hr Juni 2002,
under: http://www.medjugorje.hr/de/phanomen-medjugorje/fuhrer/ (retrieved
on 28 March 2019).

Entrance to the Garden through the Mother´s Village

Map of the Garden

Statue of Jesus Christ near the amphitheatre

The amphitheatre in the Garden

12. Communities

People who seek to lead a secular, consecrated life to God, can find the community **"Oasis of Peace"** [90]and the **"Community of the Beatitudes"** in Medjugorje. [91]

The chapel of the community can also be used by pilgrim groups for Holy Masses.

---

[90] Medjugorje Deutschland e.V.: „*Gemeinschaft "Oase des Friedens"* in medjugorje.de, unter:
https://www.medjugorje.de/medjugorje/gemeinschaften/oase-des-friedens/
(retrieved on 2019).

Comunita Mariana "Oasi della Pace"
Casa Generalizia
Casella Postale 25
I-02036 Passo Corese
Tel.: 0039-765-488993

Marijanska Zajednica "Oaza Mira"
Bijakovići
BiH-88266 Medjugorje
Bosnien-Herzegowina
Email: oaza-mira*(Bitte entfernen)*@tel.net*(Bitte entfernen)*.ba
Tel.: 00387-36-651829

[91] Medjugorje Deutschland e.V.: „*Gemeinschaft der `Seligpreisungen"* in medjugorje.de, under:
https://www.medjugorje.de/medjugorje/gemeinschaften/seligpreisungen/
(retrieved on 21 April 2019).

Gemeinschaft der Seligpreisungen
Ostwall 5
D-47589 Uedem
Tel: 02825 / 53 58 71
Fax: 02825 / 53 58 72
uedem@seligpreisungen.org

Community of the Beatitudes
Regina Pacis
BiH-88266 Medjugorje
E - mail: foyer.medjugorje*(Bitte entfernen)*@gmail *(Bitte entfernen)*.com
Tel. 00387-36 65 17 52

The **"Community Mary, Queen of Peace"**,[92] runs an encounter centre in the vicinity of the cemetery. Young people, in particular, can get guidance here. Pilgrim groups are also invited to pray and talk

"The Community Merciful Father" [93] supports young people, who are struggling with drug - and alcohol addiction.

---

[92] Medjugorje Deutschland e.V.: *Gemeinschaft „Maria, Königin des Friedens"* in medjugorje.de, under:
https://www.medjugorje.de/medjugorje/gemeinschaften/maria koenigin-des-friedens/ (retrieved on 21 April 2019).
Haus der Begegnung
Put Kovačici 26
88266 Međugorje
Tel.: +38763 356529
Mail: hausderbegegnung@maria-frieden.at

[93] Medjugorje Deutschland e.V.: *Gemeinschaft des „Barmherzigen Vaters"* in medjugorje.de, under:
https://www.medjugorje.de/medjugorje/gemeinschaften/barmherziger-vater/ (retrieved on 21 April 2019).

Präsident: Fra Svetozar Kraljevic Bijakoviči
88266 Medjugorje
Bosna i Hercegovina
Tel/Fax: +387-36-653-058
E - Mail: motac@tel.net.ba
Website: http://www.milosrdni-otac.com

THE VISIONARIES

1.   Ivanka Ivanković - Elez

The visionary was born in Bijakovići on the 21 June 1966. She was the first to see the Mother of God. Ivanka received the tenth secret on 7 May 1985. Since then, the Gospa appears to her on a yearly basis on every 25 June. She was married in 1986 and lives with her family in Medjugorje. She prays for the families.[94]

2.   Vicka Ivanović - Mijatović

Vicka is a cousin of Ivanka and was born in Bijakovići on 3 September 1964. She received nine secrets. She has been married since 2002 and has a daughter and a son. Nowadays Vicka lives near Medjugorje, in Krehin Gradac. She continues to have regular visions of the Blessed Mother. [95] She was advised to pray for the sick. The seer is at times seriously ill and thus, now seldomly meets with pilgrims. It should be noted that Vicka was allowed to write down the life of the Blessed Mother. The book is published at the behest of the Gospa. [96] The Ivanović family also received 2 antique rosaries from the Blessed Mother. [97]

3.   Mirjana Dragicević - Soldo

Mirjana was born in Sarajevo on 18 March 1965. She received all ten secrets. Mirjana is married and lives with her family in Medjugorje. Since 25 December 1982, the

---

[94] Angela Mahmoodzada u. Beatrix Zureich, *Medjugorje Kurzbericht*, 1. Aufl., Miriam Verlag, 79798 Jestetten, 2010, pp. 24 - 25.

[95] Angela Mahmoodzada u. Beatrix Zureich, *Mdejugorje Kurzbericht*, 1. Aufl., Miriam Verlag, 79798 Jestetten, 2010, p. 22.

[96] Mario Vasilj, *MEDJUGORJE APOSTELN DER GOSPA VICKA BEZEUGT*, Zweigstelle der Zentrale Hrvatska in Čitluk (Herausgeber) 2015, p. 29.

[97] Mario Vasilj, *MEDJUGORJE APOSTELN DER GOSPA VICKA BEZEUGT*, Zweigstelle der Zentrale Hrvatska in Čitluk (editor) 2015, pp. 66, 67.

Blessed Mother appears to her regularly on every 18th March. Additionally, Mirjana heard the voice of the Gospa on every 2nd of the month, since 2. August 1987. Sometimes Our Lady appeared to her as well on that occasion. The visionary experienced these encounters with the Virgin Mary in public and at the Blue Cross. Since 2008 all monthly messages were publicised.[98] Since 18 March 2020, these public apparitions on the 2nd of each month have ended. [99] Mirjana prays especially for the people who are still far from the love of God.[100]

4.   Ivan Dragicecvić

Ivan was born in Bijakovići on the 25 May 1965. Ivan received nine secrets. Although he has been married to an American and lives with his family in Boston, U.S., he spends several months every year in Medjugorje. He still has daily apparitions.[101] Ivan was asked to pray particularly for young people and priests. He also leads a prayer group, which occasionally meets at the Blue Cross.[102] The visionary has sometimes spontaneous apparitions at the Blue Cross. Most lodgings usually publicise them.

---

[98] Angela Mahmoodzada u. Beatrix Zureich, *Medjugorje Kurzbericht*, 1. Aufl., Miriam Verlag, 79798 Jestetten, 2010, p. 25.

[99] Stephen Ryan:„*Visionary Mirjana's apparitions with the Blessed Mother on the 2nd of the month have permanently ended. Will appear to Mirjana once a year on her birthday.*", in MYSTIC POST 18. März 2020, under: https://mysticpost.com/2020/03/visionary-mirjanas-apparitions-with-the-blessed-mother-on-the-2nd-of-the-month-has-permanently-ended-will-appear-to-mirjana-once-a-year-on-her-birthday/ (abgerufen am 2. April 2020).

[100] Angela Mahmoodzada u. Beatrix Zureich, *Medjugorje Kurzbericht*, 1. Aufl., Miriam Verlag, 79798 Jestetten, 2010, p. 32.

[101] Angela Mahmoodzada u. Beatrix Zureich, *Medjugorje Kurzbericht*, 1. Aufl., Miriam Verlag, 79798 Jestetten, 2010, p. 23.

[102] Angela Mahmoodzada u. Beatrix Zureich, *Mdejugorje Kurzbericht*, 1. Aufl., Miriam Verlag, 79798 Jestetten, 2010, p. 23.

5.   Ivan Ivanković

Since Ivan Ivanković does no longer have apparitions, he isn´t in the public eye anymore.

6.   Milka Pavlović

The same is true for Milka Pavlović. She is also no longer in the public eye.

7.   Marija Pavlović - Lunetti

Marija was born in Bijakovići on 1 April 1965. [103] Mother Mary has entrusted her with nine secrets. Messages of the Blessed Mother were transmitted through Marija every Thursday until 1987. Since 25 January 1987, the visionary transmits a message to the world on every 25th of the month. Unfortunately, it is difficult to be present at these apparitions, as Marija usually experiences them at her own "Magnificat Complex". In 1993 she married an Italian and lives with her children in Monza, in the vicinity of Milan, Italy. She was asked to pray for the poor souls. [104]

8.   Jakov Čolo

The visionary was born in Sarajevo on 6 March 1971. [105] He received the 10th secret on 12 September 1998. Since then Mother Mary appears to him yearly on 25 December. In 1993 he got married to an Italian and lives with his family in Medjugorje. He leads a prayer group for children and prays, upon request of Our Lady, especially for the pilgrims and the sick. [106] About Jakov Čolo the following is also to be

---

[103] Pansion Jasna, 2010, under: http://pansion-jasna.com/about%20medjugorje.html (retrieved on 21 April 2019).
[104] Angela Mahmoodzada u. Beatrix Zureich, *Medjugorje Kurzbericht*, 1. Aufl., Miriam Verlag, 79798 Jestetten, 2010, p. 23.
[105] Pansion Bell, under: http://medjugorje-81.com/vidioci/jakov-colo/?lang=en (retrieved on 21 April 2019).
[106] Angela Mahmoodzada u. Beatrix Zureich, *Medjugorje Kurzbericht*, 1. Aufl., Miriam Verlag, 79798 Jestetten, 2010, p. 24.

said: At the time of the apparitions, Jakov was only ten years old, his mother deceased and his father was working abroad. The Virgin Mary asked Jakov to deliver to Father Jozo that she wishes the prayer of the Holy Rosary.[107] The Blessed Mother also requested that Vicka should discontinue her school education and take care of Jakov. Vicka followed this instruction.[108]

9.   Jelena Vasilj - Valente

Jelena Vasilj - Valente claims to hear the voice of the Mother of God from within since 1982.[109]

10.   Marijana Vasilj - Juricić

Marijana Vasilj - Juricić also claims to preceive the voice of Our Lady from within.since 1982.[110]

STATEMENT BY THE CHURCH

Despite the strong intercession of Pope John Paul II, Medjugorje has not yet been fully recognised by the Vatican. John Paul II even mentioned towards Mirjana, at a meeting in Castel Gandolfo, that "If I wasn´t Pope, I would have been to Medjugorje a long time ago" and "that it was

---

[107] Stephen Ryan: „*Medjugorje The Little Boy Who Talks to the Celestial Mother of God Made the Rosary Come to the Church in Medjugorje*" in MYSTIC POST 2 February 2018, under: https://mysticpost.com/2018/02/little-boy-talks-celestial-mother-god-made-rosary-come-church-medjugorje/ (retrieved on 21 April 2019).

[108] Stephen Ryan:„*Medjugorje: The Strange Rosary of 7 Beads that Our Lady Says Helps Free Souls from Purgatory*", in MYSTIC POST 19 Oktober 2018, under: https://mysticpost.com/2018/10/the-strange-rosary-of-7-beads-that-our-lady-says-helps-free-souls-from-purgatory/ (retrieved on 26 March 2019).

[109] Angela Mahmoodzada u. Beatrix Zureich, *Medjugorje Kurzbericht*, 1. Aufl., Miriam Verlag, 79798 Jestetten 2010, pp. 25 - 27.

[110] Angela Mahmoodzada u. Beatrix Zureich, *Medjugorje Kurzbericht*, 1. Aufl., Miriam Verlag, 79798 Jestetten 2010, pp. 25 – 27.

the hope for the entire world"[111] In 2010, Pope Benedict XVI initiated, under the direction of Cardinal Camillo Ruini, a Congregation for the Doctrine of the Faith. This Congregation distinguished between the apparitions of the 80s and the later ones. The Ruini Congregation for the Doctrine of the Faith classified the initial apparitions as credible.[112] On 31 May 2018 Pope Francis appointed the Polish Archbishop Henryk Hoser as Apostolic Visitator for the parish of Medjugorje. Hoser came to a similar verdict as the Ruini Congregation.[113]

Until a final papal verdict is reached, Medjugorje remains recognised as a place of worship.[114] Catholics are, however, not allowed to seek contact to the seers and to attend Marian apparitions.[115] Nevertheless, there is now a positive turnaround on the part of the Vatican. Since 13 May 2019, Medjugorje pilgrims have the blessing of Pope Francis.[116] Three months later, senior Vatican representatives were sent to the Youth Festival in Medjugorje, which was thus

---

[111] kath-zdw.ch/forum/index.php?topic=4748.0 (retrieved on 2 February 2018 by "Fesa", based on the book *"Gespräch mit den Sehern"* Verlag Tiberias 2009.
[112] ERZDIÖZESE WIEN, Franziskus skeptisch zu neuen Medjugorje-Erscheinungen, in Katholische Kirche Erzdiözese Wien 15. Mai 2017, under: https://www.erzdioezese-wien.at/site/nachrichtenmagazin/schwerpunkt/papstfranziskus/article/57124.html (retreved on 23 April 2019).
[113] Dicasterium pro Communicatione, *Franziskus entsendet Visitator nach Medjugorje* in VATICAN NEWS 2017-2019, under: https://www.vaticannews.va/de/papst/news/2018-05/franziskus-entsendet-visitator-medjugorje-hoser.html (retrieved on 23 April 2019).
[114] Totus Tuus – Neuevangelisierung e.V., Mit Totus Tuus nach Medjugorje, in Totus Tuus 2005-2018 under: http://www.totus-tuus.de/site/medjugorje/mit-totus-tuus-nach-medjugorje/ (retrieved on 23 April 2019).
[115] Felizitas Küble, *Vatikan untersagt Katholiken Teilnahme an Pro-Medjugorje-Versammlungen* in kathnews Rom und die Welt 20. März 2015, under: http://www.kathnews.de/vatikan-untersagt-katholiken-teilnahme-an-pro-medjugorje-versammlungen (retrieved on 23 April 2019).
[116] Independent.ie: „*Pope finally gives his blessing to Medjugorje pilgrims*" unter: https://www.independent.ie/world-news/europe/pope-finally-gives-his-blessing-to-medjugorje-pilgrims-38104871.html (retrieved on 18. May 2019).

officially recognised for the first time. This is understood as another approval of the apparition site.[117]

HOW TO GET TO MEDJUGORJE?

The easiest way to get to Medjugorje is by plane. Possible airports are the tourist destinations Zadar, Split and Dubrovnik. From there, you can then cross the long border area by car. You can also take the night bus from Dubrovnik.[118] It is ideal, however, to catch a flight to Mostar (OMO). The airport is only about 20 kilometres away from Medjugorje[119]. According to the airport´s website, it serves the following airlines:[120]:

◆ AlMasria Universal Airlines

◆ Aeolian Airlines

◆ Alitalia

◆ Helitt Lineas Aereas

◆ Livingston

◆ Meridiana

◆ Mistral Air

◆ Small Planet Airlines

---

[117] Jonathan Luxmoore CATHOLIC NEWS SERVICE: „*Vatican confirms Medjugorje approval by joining youth festival*" *in* CRUX Taking the Catholic Pulse 7. August 2019, under: https://cruxnow.com/church-in-europe/2019/08/vatican-confirms-medjugorje-approval-by-joining-youth-festival/ (retrieved on 15 March 2020).

[118] Rome2rio, under: https://www.rome2rio.com/map/Munich-Airport-MUC/Medjugorje (retrieved on 23 April 2019).

[119] https://www.mytrip.com/ (retrieved on 4 May 2019).

[120] http://mostar-airport.ba/en/ (retrieved on 4.May 2019).

◆Neos

◆Trade Air

This information is provided without any warranty.

POSSIBLE CONTACT TO THE VISIONARIES

It is not necessary to go on an organised to, in order to encounter a visionary. You can, for example, simply attend a Marian Apparition.

It is also possible to contact the visionaries through the Information Centre.

The following pensions/hotels are also owned by the seers (which doesn´t mean that one necessarily meets the visionaries):

1. **Pansion DH Dragicević** in Bijakovići, Medjugorje [121]

    Tel: + 387 (0) 36650389
    E - mail: info@travel-medjugorje.com

2. **Pansion Stana,** is situated only 50 metres away from St. James´Church.

---

[121] Whl travel: *Pansion Dragevic* in: Medjugorje Tours and Travel 2016, under: https://www.travel-medjugorje.com/Pension_Dragicevic (retrieved on 21 April 2019).

Pape Ivana Paula II 20, 88266 Medjugorje
E-mail: pansion@medjugorje-stana.com [122]
Tel: + 387 36 833 832

3.   **The Magnificat Centre** [123]
The Centre is a hotel/restaurant complex under the
management of Marija Pavlović - Lunetti. She
occasionally receives her messages at this centre, in
the presence of pilgrims.

Ulica Kraljice Mira 106,
Bijakovići, BiH-88266 Medjugorje,
Tel: + 387.36.650359, + 387.36.653809-10
Fax: + 387.36.653811
E-mail: magnificatcenter2014@gmail.com
http://www.magnificat.center/?lang=en

4.   **Jakov Colos Pansion Bell** [124]

Ilke Baraća 32,
88266 Međugorje
E-mail: tvukosav@net.hr

---

[122] Hotel Stana, under: http://medjugorje-stana.com/ (retrieved on 21. April 2019).

[123] Magnificat Center, 2016 - 2017, under:
http://www.magnificat.center/?lang=en (retrieved on 21 April 2019).

[124] Medjugorje - 81.com: *Pansion Bell* under: http://medjugorje-81.com/vidioci/jakov-colo/?lang=en (retrieved on 21 April 2019).

Tel: + 387 36 650 141
Fax: + 387 36 651 141[125]
http://medjugorje-81.com/vidioci/jakov-colo/?lang=e

In addition, I was able to find the following tour operators which enable a proximity to the visionaries.

1. **Dragićević Family House Pilgrimages,** (with Ivan as a host) organised by
206 Tours Inc.[126]

   333 Marcus Blvd.
   Hauppauge, NY 11788
   Tel: 1-800-206-TOUR (8687)
   E-mail sales@206tours.com
   http://www.pilgrimages.com/medj/

2. **Magnificat Tours (with Mirjana as host)** [127]

   983 E. Rojo Way Gilbert, AZ 85297
   Tel.: 480.726.8611
   Tel.: 877.333.9290

3. **Mafegeni Viaggi (encounter with Vicka)** [128]

   Via Bagnolo 14, Tavazzana (LO) Italy
   Tel: 02.39523309 | 02.395233
   (Mon - Fri: 9.00-18.00)

---

[125] Medjugorje -81.com: *Pansion Bell* under: http://medjugorje-81.com/vidioci/jakov-colo/?lang=en (retrieved on 21 April 2019).
[126] http://www.pilgrimages.com/medj/ (retrieved on 4 May 2019).
[127] http://www.magnificattours.com/medjugorje-tour-dates.php (retrieved on 4 May 2019).
[128] https://www.pellegrinaggisanti.com/club-magellano/ (retrieved on 4. May 2019).

Tel: (prefix for Italy: 0039) 327.1493890 (available 24 h)

Annotation: Pilgrims, who "only" need pastoral care, can contact the Information Centre. It facilitates the contact to the Franciscan friars and to priests.[129]

RELEVANT YOU TUBE VIDEOS

1.   **Experience Medjugorje and Our Lady's Messages**
Published by: Janet Moore

   Published on: 9 March 2018 [130]

2.   **Fr. Slavko - why Our Lady says constantly, "pray, pray, pray!"**
Published by: MarytvMedjugorje
Published on: 19 March 2011 [131]

3.   **Mary TV Medjugorje** [132]

4.   **Sister Emmanuel Maillard** [133]

5.   **Fr. Donald Calloway-"Medjugorje: A Call to Priesthood"** 2004
Published by: ebaytimr [134]

---

[129] Medjugorje WebSite: „*Information Centre "Mir" Medjugorje*" in www.medjugorje.hr 10. November 2006, under: https://www.medjugorje.ws/en/apparitions/docs-information-center-mir-medjugorje/ (retrieved on 4 May 2019).

[130] https://www.youtube.com/watch?v=QUwVvuPr87Q (retrieved on 4 May 2019).

[131] https://www.youtube.com/watch?v=5IfP_QcSEcg (retrieved on 21 April 2019).

[132] https://www.youtube.com/results?search_query=mary+tv+medjugorje+live (retrieved on 2.April 2019).

[133] https://www.youtube.com/channel/UCveRmNCjId_yX6zkqz9VEbQ (abgerufen am: 21 April 2019).

[134] https://www.youtube.com/watch?v=GKg3BOfEB6g (retrieved on 21 April 2019).

Published on: 21 September 2017

6. **Medjugorje i.e.**[135]

7. **Father Peter Rookey Healing Service Medjugorje May 12 1991**
Published by: ebaytimr [136]
Published on: 1 February 2015

8. **Statue of Risen Christ in Medjugorje weeping**
Published by: israelsheli
Published on: 29 October 2014.[137]

9. **The statue of the "Risen Christ" in Medjugorje - Miraculous water - Healings**
Published by: CroixAcier.fr
Published on: 15 June 2017 [138]

10. **Medjugorje - Amazing healing testimony!**
Fr. Peter Glas, Episode 68, Fruit of Medjugorje
Published by: Mary TV Medjugorje
Published on: 22 May 2013 [139]

11. **The Medjugorje Visionaries - the scientific tests**
Published by: davidtlig
Published on: 8 February 2016 [140]

12. **Our Lady´s Message of Fasting - Father Slavko Barbarić** Medjugorje June 1990
Published by: catholicfocus
Published on: 30 March 2013 [141]

13. **Objections to Medjugorje**
Published by: Our Lady at Medjugorje

---

[135] https://www.youtube.com/results?search_query=Medjugorje+i.e. (retrieved on 21 April 2019).

[136] https://www.youtube.com/watch?v=8M0YIfUDEDs (retrieved on 21 April 2019).

[137] https://www.youtube.com/watch?v=fLOgYxLYz9A (retrieved on 21 April 2019).

[138] https://www.youtube.com/watch?v=4_bfNCJTF3Q (retrieved on 21 April 2019).

[139] https://www.youtube.com/watch?v=Nps5VCb14jg (retrieved on 21 April 2019).

[140] https://www.youtube.com/watch?v=X4YDn7ccl3g (retrieved on 21 April 2019).

[141] https://ww.youtube.com/watch?v=CfrrPvnG9ho (retrieved on 30 March 2019).

Published on: 25 September 2018 [142]

14. The Miracle of Medjugorje in english (sic!)
Published by: estohacelperu (Film of „D & J
PRODUCTION", © 2005 Copyright, The Miracle of
Medjugorje, English version.
Published on: 8 September 2018 [143]

**15. Some Messages Seem Contrary to the Catholic
Faith**
Published by: Tekton Ministries
Published on: 20 September 2019 [144]

**<u>Annotation:</u> All You Tube information is provided
without warranty. In the unfortunate event of a change
in content, I cannot be held accountable.**

SUBJECT - RELATED DVDs

1. Mary's Land: And if it isn´t a miracle?
Juan Manuel Cotelo (director), 2017

2. The Triumph, 2013

3. Apparition Hill, 2017
Stella Mar Films

---

[142] https://www.youtube.com/watch?v=u3Jo-67tsw4 (retrieved on 30 March
2019).
[142]

https://www.youtube.com/results?search_query=Medjugorje+film (retrieved on
8 July 2019).
[144] https://www.youtube.com/watch?v=TArwTPSJ6j0 (retrieved on 4 November
2019).

BOOKS ABOUT MEDJUGORJE

1. **Books pertaining to the Messages:**

a) *The Messages of Medjugorje,*
    The Complete Text, 1981 - 2014
    Medjugorje - Apologia.com
    ISBN 978-1-304-86163-4

b) *Maria spricht in Medjugorje:* Sämtliche
    Botschaften der Gottesmutter
    Reimo Verlag (1 December 2002)
    ISBN-10: 9783980581073

c) *The Messages of Our Lady of Peace*
    Informativni centar „MIR" Medjugorje 2018
    ISBN 978-9958-36-161-6

2. **My Heart Will Triumph**
    15. August 2016
    by Mirjana Soldo (author), Sean Bloomfield
    (contributor), Miljenko Musa (contributor)
    Publisher: Catholic Shop
    ISBN-10: 0997890606

3. **I saw the Mother of God: Talks with the
    visionary Vicka in Medjugorje**
    By Janko Bubalo
    ISBN-10: 3874491757

4. **About Fasting:**

a) **Freed and Healed Through Fasting**
    by Sister Emmanuel,
    3. ed., Parvis - Publishers, 1648
    Hauteville/Switzerland, January 2013

ISBN 978-3-907525-64-7

b)   **FASTING**
by Pater Dr. Slavko Barbarić OFM
Medjugorje - book series volume 1
1991
Missionary Press St. Gabriel
2340 Mödling

c)   **FASTING**
by Father Slavko Barbarić, O.F.M.
Informativni centar, MIR" Medjugorje 2018
(originally published in 1988 by Franciscan
University Press, Steubenville, OH, USA),
ISBN: 978-9958-36-002-2

5.   **The Ten Secrets of the Blessed Virgin Mary**
by Dan Lynch

6.   **Medjugorje Kurzbericht**
by Angela Mahmoodzada and Beatrix Zureich,
1. edition, Miriam Publishers, 79798 Jestetten, 2010
Germany
ISBN: 978-3-87449-367-3

7.   **Medjugorje - ein gesegnetes Land**
Armand Girard - Guy Girard - Janko Bubalo, 1990,
Miriam Publishers, 79798 Jestetten, Germany
ISBN: 3-87449-191-9

8.   **The Stations of the Cross**
von Pater Slavko Barbarić, O.F.M.
Informativni centar „MIR" Medjugorje 2017
ISBN: 978-9958-36-176-0

9.   **Give Me Your Wounded Heart**, A Guide for
Confession
by Pater Slavko Barbarić, O.F.M.

Paraclete Pr 1. October 1991
ISBN: 978-1557250230

10. **Medjugorje Apostles of the Gospa Mirjana testifies**
By Mario Vasilj, Čitluk - Medjugorje 2015, Ogranak
Matice hrvatske u Čitluku
ISBN: 978-9958-831-607

11. **Medjugorje Magazine, Prayer Action Maria – Queeen of Peace**
By Gebetsaktion Medjugorje,
Postbox 18, 1153 Vienna, Austria
Tel: +43 1 8939007 (Mon - Fr: 9.00 - 12.00 Uhr)

MEDJUGORJE - MUSIC

1. **Adoration music by the group "Figli del Divino Amore"**

   E-mail: dim_cielo@yahoo.com
   www.figlideldivinoamore.org

PRAYERS

1. THE HAIL MARY [145]

"Hail Mary, full of grace, the Lord is with thee.
Blessed art thou amongst women, and blessed is the fruit of

---

[145] Medjugorje, Geschichte, Gebete, Botschaften, Stadtplan, p. 36. (translation
into English: the author)

thy womb, Jesus.
Holy Mary, Mother of God, pray for us sinners, now and at
the hour of our death. Amen."

2.   The Lord´s Prayer [146]

"Our Father, who art in Heaven, hallowed be Thy name,
Thy Kingdom come, Thy will be done, on earth as it is in
heaven. Give us this day our daily bread. And forgive us our
trespasses, as we forgive those who trespass against us.
And lead us not into temptation, but deliver us from evil.
For Thine is the kingdom, and the power, and the glory,
for ever and ever. Amen."

3.   Glory be to the Father [147]

"Glory be to the Father and to the Son and to the Holy
Spirit. As it was in the beginning is now, and ever shall be,
world without end. Amen."

4.   The Apostles´ Creed [148]

---

[146] Medjugorje, Geschichte, Gebete, Botschaften, Stadtplan, p. 36. (translation into English: the author)

[147] (Erz-)Bischöfen Deutschlands und Österreichs und dem Bischof von Bozen-Brixen, *Gotteslob Katholisches Gebet- und Gesangbuch Ausgabe für die Diözese Würzburg*, Katholische Bibelanstalt GmbH, Stuttgart and Echter Publisher and Printing Press C.H. Beck, Nördlingen 2013, Germany, p. 35. (translation into English: the author)

[148] (Erz-)Bischöfen Deutschlands und Österreichs und dem Bischof von Bozen-Brixen, *Gotteslob Katholisches Gebet- und Gesangbuch Ausgabe für die Diözese Würzburg*, Katholische Bibelanstalt GmbH, Stuttgart and Echter Publisher and Printing Press C.H. Beck, Nördlingen 2013, Germany, p. 36. (translation into English the author)

"I believe in God,/ the Father Almighty,/ Creator of Heaven
and earth,/ and in Jesus Christ,/ His only Son, our Lord,/
who was conceived by the Holy Spirit,/ born of the Virgin
Mary,/ suffered under Pontius Pilate,/ was crucified, died
and was buried,/ He descended into hell,/ on the third day
He rose again from the dead,/ He ascended into heaven;/
and is seated at the right hand of God the Father Almighty;/
from there He will come to judge the living and the dead./
I believe in the Holy Spirit,/ the Holy Catholic Church,/
the communion of Saints,/ the forgiveness of sins,/ the
resurrection of the body, and life everlasting./ Amen."

5.   The Holy Rosary

Before I expand on the Rosary as such, I would like to point
briefly to the history of the Holy Rosary
The prayer of the Rosary is said to have emerged from a
vision of the Mother of God to St. Dominic (Toulouse,
France), as a "weapon", for the conversion of sinners and
the Albigensians (with success!!!) [149]

The Catholic Hymn Book explains the significance of the
prayer of the Holy Rosary as follows: "Means and end of
the prayer of the Rosary is Jesus Christ, the Son of God.
Together with the Virgin Mary we look at His life. She
knew Jesus, like no other human being; she accompanied
Him to all important stations of His life - until under the
Cross. In her, the power of the resurrection became visible:
She was received into the glory of God - which is a sign of
hope for the Church and for all people.

In the sentences of the Rosary – which are the clauses that
extend the `Hail Mary´ - we look at the secrets of the Faith.

---

[149] theholyrosary.org: *„THE HOLY ROSARY"* in: theholyrosary.org 2019 under:
http://www.theholyrosary.org/rosaryhistory (retrieved on 20. March 2019).

Repeating the same sentences gives us peace of mind. The beads of the Holy Rosary aid in praying:" [150]

The Rosary consists of a cross and 59 pearls.

The prayer of the Rosary begins with the Sign of the Cross: In the name of the Father and the Son and the Holy Spirit. Amen.

"At the cross", one prays "the Creed" and "the Glory be to the Father".

At the 1s pearl after the cross, one prays "the Our Father".

At the pearls 2 – 4 after the cross, 3 "Hail Mary´s" are prayed[151] for the following intentions:

1)   the intention of faith

2)   the intention of hope

3)   the intention of love

At the 4th pearl after the cross, the "Our Father" is prayed once again. [152]

Then "follow ten 'Hail Mary' at a time with the insertion of a mystery (... and blessed is the fruit of your body, Jesus whom you, O Virgin, have conceived by the Holy Spirit).

---

[150] (Erz-)Bischöfen Deutschlands und Österreichs und dem Bischof von Bozen-Brixen, *Gotteslob Katholisches Gebet- und Gesangbuch Ausgabe für die Diözese Würzburg*, Katholische Bibelanstalt GmbH, Stuttgart und Echter Verlag und Druckerei C.H. Beck, Nördlingen 2013, Germany, p. 38. (translation into English: the author)

[151] This part of the citation from the German Cathoic Hymn Book has been altered, to match the English practice of the prayer of the Holy Rosary.

[152] (Erz-)Bischöfen Deutschlands und Österreichs und dem Bischof von Bozen-Brixen, *Gotteslob Katholisches Gebet- und Gesangbuch Ausgabe für die Diözese Würzburg*, Katholische Bibelanstalt GmbH, Stuttgart und Echter Verlag und Druckerei C.H. Beck, Nördlingen 2013, Germany, pp. 38 - 39. (translation into English: the author)

The completion of each sentence is concluded with the "Glory to the Father..."

The contemplation of the next mystery is opened again with an "Our Father".

The Joyful Mysteries (M, Sa and Su during advent and at Christmas) [153]

1. whom thou, O virgin, hast conceived from the Holy Spirit

2. whom thou, O Virgin, hast borne to Elizabeth

3. whom thou, O Virgin, hast born in Bethlehem

4. whom thou, O Virgin, hast sacrificed in the temple

5. whom thou, O Virgin, hast found again in the temple

The Luminous Mysteries (Th)

1. who was baptised by John the Babtist

2. who revealed himself at the wedding in Cana

3. who has proclaimed the Kingdom of God

4. who was transfigured on the mountain

---

[153] The days of prayer are based on a recommendation of John Paul II: Source: Rosary Center. „HOW TO PRAY THE ROSARY" in: Rosary Center 2020 under: https://www.rosarycenter.org/homepage-2/rosary/how-to-pray-the-rosary/ (retrieved on 23 March 2020).

5. who has given us the Holy Eucharist

The Sorrowful Mysteries (T, F and Su during Lent)

1. who sweated blood for us

2. who was scourged for us

3. who has been crowned with thorns for us

4. who has carried the heavy cross for us

5. who has been crucified for us

The Glorious Mysteries (W and Su in general)

1. who has risen from the dead

2. who has ascended to Heaven

3. who has sent us the Holy Spirit

4. who you, O Virgin, has welcomed you into Heaven

5. who you, O Virgin, has crowned you in Heaven

The Comforting Mysteries

1. who reigns as King

2. who rules and works in His Church

3. who will return in glory

4. who will judge the living and the dead

5. who will complete everything" [154]

[154] (Erz-)Bischöfen Deutschlands und Österreichs und dem Bischof von Bozen-Brixen, *Gotteslob Katholisches Gebet- und Gesangbuch Ausgabe für die Diözese Würzburg*, Katholische Bibelanstalt GmbH, Stuttgart und Echter Verlag und Druckerei C.H. Beck, Nördlingen 2013, Germany, pp. 39 – 40. (translation into English: the author)

6.   Oh my Jesus (Fatima - Prayer) [155]

"O my Jesus, forgive us our sins, save us from the fires of Hell, and lead all souls to Heaven, especially those in most need of Your Mercy. Amen." [156]

7.   Fatima - Prayer transmitted by the Angel of Peace

"My God, I believe, I adore, I hope and I love You! I ask pardon of You for those who do not believe, do not adore, do not hope and do not love You!" [157] (3x)

8.   The Medjugorje Chaplet [158]

In Medjugorje, prayer beads which are shorter than the ordinary Rosary beads are sold. This type of Rosary serves the veneration of the wounds of Jesus Christ. Included in these wounds are the wounds at his shoulder, and those caused by the crown of thorns.
This string of beads has its origin in an old Bosnian and Herzegovinian tradition. One prays 7 Our Father, 7 Hail Mary and 7 Glory Be to the Father.
In the Message from 3 July 1981, Our Lady asked the seers to pray the Apostles´ Creed ahead of the Chaplet.

---

[155] Medjugorje, Geschichte, Gebete, Botschaften, Stadtplan, p. 38.
[156] The prayer goes back to the third apparition in Fatima in 1917: It is a prayer of penance and a prayer for the deceased. It has no papal approval.
Wikipedia.org, „Fatima-Gebet" under: https://de.wikipedia.org/wiki/Fatima-Gebet (retrieved on 26 March 2019).
[157] Severo Rossi, *Fátima Ort der Haoffnung und des Friedens*, 5. Aufl., CONSOLATA EDITORA PORTUGAL, 10. June 1997, p. 10.
[158] Stephen Ryan: *„ Medjugorje: The Strange Rosary of 7 Beads that Our Lady Says Helps Free Souls from Purgatory"*, in MYSTIC POST 19. October 2018, under: https://mysticpost.com/2018/10/the-strange-rosary-of-7-beads-that-our-lady-says-helps-free-souls-from-purgatory/ (retrieved on 26 March 2019).

According to Message of 20 July 20 1982, Our Lady added
that this prayer was especially useful for the poor souls in

On the recommendation of Mother Mary, it has also become
customary to pray the Chaplet after every holy Mass, as a
means of thanksgiving.

9.　　The Chaplet of Divine Mercy [159]

(prayed with an ordinary Rosary)

"Begin with:

The Our Father, Hail Mary, Apostles' Creed

On the big beads (once)

Eternal Father, I offer you the Body and Blood, Soul and
Divinity of Your Dearly Beloved Son, Our Lord, Jesus
Christ, in atonement for our sins and those of the whole
world.

On the small beads (ten times):

For the sake of His sorrowful Passion, have mercy on us
and on the whole world.

At the end (thrice):

Holy God, Holy Mighty One, Holy Immortal One, have
mercy on us and on the whole world. Amen.

---

[159] Fr. Seraphim Michalenko, MIC and Vinny Flynn und Robert A. Stackpole,
The Divine Mercy Message and Devotion, Revised Edition, MARIAN PRESS,
Stockbridge MA 01263, U.S.A., 2008, pp. 65 - 67.

Optional Closing Prayer (thrice):

"Eternal God, in whom mercy is endless and the treasury of
compassion is inexhaustible, look kindly upon us and
increase Your mercy in us, that in difficult moments we
might not despair nor become despondent, but with
great confidence submit ourselves to Your holy will,
which is Love and Mercy itself. "

10.   Consecraton Prayer to the Most Holy Trinity through Mother Mary [160] [161]

"Mary, You have invited us to consecrate ourselves to Your
Immaculate Heart. I know that You want to lead us to God,
because You love us infinitely and want us to be content.

Today I would like to answer Your invitation.
Just like Jesus gave you to me on the cross, I will also give
myself to you. Into Your hands I renew my baptismal
promise and consecrate myself to Your Immaculate Heart in
order to belong completely to the Most Holy Trinity. I give
You my heart, my soul, my spirit and my body, my talents
and gifts, my past, present and future.

Take me into Your arms and help me, to love Jesus the way
You love him! From You I want to learn, to listen to the
Word of the Father and to do His Will.

---

[160] Community of the Beautitudes, House Regina Pacis – Post Box 16, 8826
Medjugorje – Bijakovići, flyer.
[161] No special reference is made to the insertion of punctuation marks by the
author.

Like You Mary, I request to receive the Holy Spirit into my heart.

Together with You, Mary, I want to learn to love all people, as they all belong to Jesus. I consecrate myself to You, that my prayer may be a prayer with the heart, through which I find peace, joy and love, and the strength to reconcile with my fellow men.

I also consecrate to You my family, my friends and all people, especially those who need the help and mercy of God the most.

Like Jesus I want to live every day at Your side. From now on everything in me shall praise my Lord! May my heart rejoice in God my Saviour!"

PRAYER PROGRAMME [162]

In the mornings: Holy Mass in different languages
In the afternoons: Silent Adoration in Adoration Chapel

	1. Sept. – 31. Mai	1. Juni – 31. Aug
Evening Prayer Programme and Confession	17h - 20h 17h Joyful and Sorrowful Mysteries of the Rosary 18h Holy Mass, blessing of objects, prayer for health, Glorious Mysteries of the Rosary	18h - 21h 18h Joyful and Sorrowful Mysteries of the Rosary 19h Holy Mass, blessing of objects, prayer for health, Glorious Mysteries of the Rosary
Eucha-ristic Adoration	Tu and Sa 21h - 22h Th 19h - 20h	Tu and Sa 22h - 23h Th 20h - 21h
Veneration of the Cross	F 19h - 20h	F 20h - 21h
Way of the Cross on Cross Mountain	F 14h	F 16h
Rosary on Apparition Hill	Su 14h	Su 16h

Holy Mass in English: weekdays at 10 a.m,

---

[162] The Prayer Programme corresponds to the information brochure of the Information Center "MIR" Medjugorje.

Sundays 12 a.m. (The Holy Masses take place alternately in St. James Church and in the Hall of Blessed John Paul II)

EXCURSIONS

1.   Šurmanci - Jesus of Divine Mercy

The village of Šurmanci is about 7,5 km outside of Medjugorje. The story of how the Divine Mercy Jesus icon got to the church of Šurmanci is one of healing. Mr. Ugo Festa, an Italian, was born in Vicenza, Italy in 195. In his early years he was diagnosed with multiple sclerosis. At the age of 39, however, he did not only suffer from multiple sclerosis, but also from epilepsy, week muscles and a deformed spine. After a reluctant pilgrimage to Lourdes, he turned to the Faith again. In 1990, Mr. Festa now relying on a wheel chair, went on a pilgrimage to Rome. There, he encountered St. Mother Teresa and Pope John Paul II. Both advised him to rely on the "Jesus of Divine Mercy" and to make a pilgrimage to the Church dedicated to "Divine Mercy" in Trent, Italy.
Mr. Festa followed the advice and went to Trent. In a side altar of the Villa O'Santissima, Villazzano, Mr. Festa then prayed for 3 consecutive days in front of this life - size icon of "Jesus of Divine Mercy". On the fourth day he was healed by Jesus himself, Who spoke to him from the picture with these words: "Rise and walk". In the same year he told Pope John Paul II about his healing. Ugo Festa spent the rest of his life as a voluntary helping the poor, sick and homeless in Italy, India and Africa.

He did this to aid the Sisters of Mother Teresa. [163] [164] At the same time, he spread the veneration of the "Jesus of Divine Mercy." In 2005, Mr. Festa was suffering from cancer. He did, however, not die of cancer, but of two bullet wounds which two strangers inflicted on him during his dangerous missionary work.[165]

At the request of the Bishop of Split, Mons. Franic, the icon was then brought to Medjugorje in an "imploring" procession by a prayer group from Trent. In Medjugorje, the ican was at first placed in Adoration Chapel.[166] The icon is now located at the Church of Šurmanci. The Church was built in 2002.[167]

The healing of Mr. Festa was noted and confirmed at the canonization of Sister Faustina. The Church in Šurmanci also houses relics of Sister Faustina[168] and of Pope John Paul II.[169]

---

[163] Medjugorje Council of Ireland, *The miraculous healing of Ugo Festa in front of a Divine Mercy Icon. Icon now in Šurmanci, Medjugorje.*in, 2016 - 2019, under: https://medjugorjecouncil.ie/miraculous-healing-ugo-festa-front-divine-mercy-icon-icon-now-surmanci-medjugorje/ (retrieved on 17 May 2019).

[164] www.medjugorjeassisi.it, *MARIA KÖNIGIN DES FRIEDENS; ŠURMANCI*; under: http://www.medjugorjeassisi.it/surmanci-en.htm (retrieved on 27.May 2019).

[165] Medjugorje Council of Ireland, *The miraculous healing of Ugo Festa in front of a Divine Mercy Icon. Icon now in Šurmanci, Medjugorje*, 2016 – 2019, under: https://medjugorjecouncil.ie/miraculous-healing-ugo-festa-front-divine-mercy-icon-icon-now-surmanci-medjugorje/ (retrieved on 17 May 2019).

[166] www.medjugorjeassisi.it, *MARIA KÖNIGIN DES FRIEDENS; ŠURMANCI*; under: http://www.medjugorjeassisi.it/surmanci-en.htm (retrieved on 27.May 2019).

[167] Udruga Međugorje - MIR, Split, HR „*Medjugorje place of prayer and reconciliation, Divine Mercy Sunday in Surmanci*" in medjugorje.hr 1995 - 2019, under: http://www.medjugorje.hr/de/phanomen- http://www.botschaften-mariens.de/cms/pater-jozo-zovko/medjugorje/erscheinungen/ (retrieved on 17 May 2019).

[168] www.medjugorjeassisi.it, *MARIA KÖNIGIN DES FRIEDENS; ŠURMANCI*; under: http://www.medjugorjeassisi.it/surmanci-en.htm (retrieved on 27.May 2019).

[169] Gloria.tv, 22.April 2017 under: https://gloria.tv/reply/b8W87SZEg2Fs6pCjyYf2ER7xB (retrieved on 17 May 2019).

Šurmanci Church

Divine Mercy - Jesus

Painting in the Šurmanci Church by Ljubo Jovanović

2. Our Lady of Tihaljina

The village of Tihaljina is about 32 km from Medjugorje. In the 50s, the parishioners bought an inexpensive Statue of Our Lady from Italy. Due to the strong charisma of the Statue, many people made a pilgrimage to Our Lady of Tihaljina. ("Our Mother of Mercy") [170].

Today one can find many depictions of the Statue in Medjugorje. There are two reasons for that:
First, the visionaries claimed that the Statue bears a strong resemblance to the Gospa of Medjugorje.
And second, after his release from prison, Father Jozo was exiled to Tihaljina.[171]

Some pilgrims also claim that when praying in front of the Statue, both the facial expression and the arm posture of Our Lady change.[172]

You can get Tihaljina by first taking the R424 (M6) from Medjugorje towards Ljubuški. From Ljubuški you continue towards Imotski. There you turn on the R42.
Alternatively, you can enter the following address into your navigational system:

Crkva Bezgrešnog začeća Blažene Djevice Marije, 88348, Bosnia and Herzegovina (Tel: + 387 39 673 - 004)

---

[170] *„Pater Jozo Zovko"* in *www.botschaften-mariens.de,* 10. December 2014, under: http://www.botschaften-mariens.de/cms/pater-jozo-zovko/ (retrieved on 26 March 2019).

[171] *„Pater Jozo Zovko"* in *www.botschaften-mariens.de,* 10. December 2014, under: http://www.botschaften-mariens.de/cms/pater-jozo-zovko/(retrieved on 26 March 2019).

[172] Medjugorje Hotel & Spa: „Surroundings of Medjugorje *Natural Wonders And Cultural Attractions"* in: Medjugorje Hotel & Spa 2017, under:
https://www.medjugorjehotelspa.com/en/medjugorje-what-to-see-in-the-surroundings/ (retrieved on 28 March 2019).

3. Koćuša Waterfalls

On your way to Tihaljina, between Vitina and Klobuk are the Koćuša - Waterfalls.
Right next to the Waterfalls is the ***Restaurant Vodopad Koćuša.***
Veljaci bb, Ljubuški 88320, Bosnia & Herzegovina
Tel: +387 63 789 789 [173]

---

[173] https://www.google.com/search?client=firefox-b-d&q=vodopad+kocusa (retrieved on 8 May 2019).

4.   Humac Museum and St. Anthony Monastery

For those interested in culture, the monastery of St. Anthony of Padua, located in Humac, is a good place to visit. The monastery is located outside of Ljubuški in the direction of Teskera and is about 13.5 km from Medjugorje.

It is the oldest monastery in all of Bosnia and Herzegovina and houses the 'Mother' Museum. In the museum you can admire the oldest document written in Croatian, namely the Humac tablet from 1185.[174]

The museum can be entered from a side entrance recessed into the ground.

[174] Medjugorje Hotel & Spa: „Surroundings of Medjugorje
Natural Wonders And Cultural Attractions " in: Medjugorje
Hotel & Spa 2017, under:
https://www.medjugorjehotelspa.com/en/medjugorje-what-to-see-in-the-surroundings/ (retrieved on 28 March 2019).

5.   Mostar

The distance between Mostar and Medjugorje is about
26 km. The city is situated on the bank of the Neretva River.
Mostar is famous for its Stari Most bridge, which dates back
to the 16th century. Unfortunately, the original bridge was
destroyed during the Bosnian War in the 90s. Today, the
bridge has been rebuilt and divides Mostar into a Muslim
and Croatian part. The Muslim part still bears strong
testimony to the Ottoman Empire. With its mosques, it is
one of the UNESCO World Heritage Sites. [175] Mostar is
also known for its "jumping competition" from the Stari
Most Bridge. It takes place every July. [176]

Apart from the world heritage, you can also find the modern
Mepas Shopping Mall in Mostar; just in case you forgot to
bring something along.

---

[175] Medjugorje Hotel & Spa: „Surroundings of Medjugorje
Natural Wonders And Cultural Attractions" in: Medjugorje
Hotel & Spa 2017, under:
https://www.medjugorjehotelspa.com/en/medjugorje-what-to-see-in-the-surroundings/ (retrieved on 28 March 2019).
[176] Amel Salihbasić, „*Komm, entdecke, erzähle weiter BOSNIEN UND
HERZEGOWINA 30 unvergessliche Tage*", 3. Ed.., Amel Salihbasić (self -
publishing), Vienna, Austria 2017, page 9.

6.   Blagaj Tekke, (a Dervisch monastery)

The Tekke is about 28 km from Medjugorje. It is in the vicinity of Mostar Airport. You can find a waterfall there, which plunges into the Buna River from a height of 200 meters. The ruins of the village of Herceg Stjepan are located above the waterfall. Below the waterfall is the Dervisch Tekij monastery, dating back from 1660.[177]

---

[177] Medjugorje Hotel & Spa: „Surroundings of Medjugorje *Natural Wonders And Cultural Attractions* " in: Medjugorje Hotel & Spa 2017, under: https://www.medjugorjehotelspa.com/en/medjugorje-what-to-see-in-the-surroundings/ (retrieved on 28 March 2019).

Blagaj Tekke

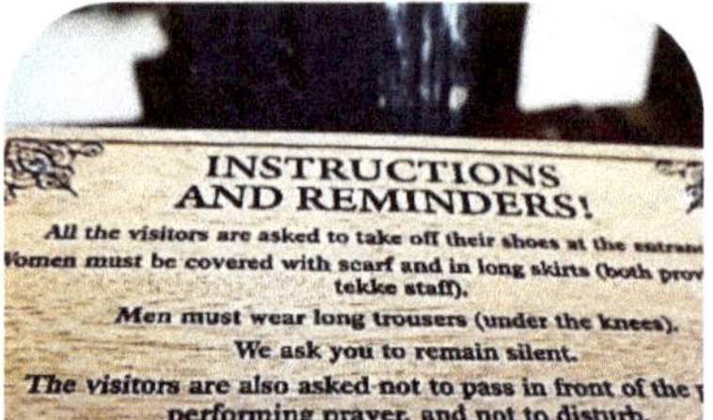

Rules of Conduct for the Tekke

7.   Die Kravice Waterfalls

Ca. 20 km von Medjugorje entfernt, liegen die einzigartigen Kravice Wasserfälle. Wenn es warm ist, kann man dort auch etwas baden.

8. Pocitelj

Another UNESCO World Heritage Site is the small town Pocitelj,. The town is at a distance of about 18 km from Medjugorje.[178]

Pocitelj was founded in 1383 by the Bosnian King Tvrtko. The architectural style of Pocitelj was at first Mediterranean. Through the invasion of the Turks, however, it was later orientalised. The town is known for its handicrafts.

---

[178] Medjugorje Hotel & Spa: „Surroundings of Medjugorje *Natural Wonders And Cultural Attractions*" in: Medjugorje Hotel & Spa 2017, under: https://www.medjugorjehotelspa.com/en/medjugorje-what-to-see-in-the-surroundings/ (retrieved on 28 March 2019).

9.   The Nature Reserve Hutovo Blato

The Hutovo Blato is a very beautiful swamp area, which is home to many species of birds and plants. The swamp is also one of the largest hibernation places for birds from Europe.[179] The Nature Reserve is about 30 km form Medjugorje.

The Hutovo Blato is suitable for relaxation and hiking. There is also a 3 - star hotel, the "Hotel Park". [180]

---

[179] Medjugorje Hotel & Spa: *„Surroundings of Medjugorje Natural Wonders And Cultural Attractions"* in: Medjugorje Hotel & Spa 2017, under:
https://www.medjugorjehotelspa.com/en/medjugorje-what-to-see-in-the-surroundings/ (retrieved on 28. March 2019).
[180] Contact:
Hotel Park, Makart Hoteli d.o.o.
Karaotok bb
Hutovo blato
88300 Čapljina
BiH
Tel.: +387 36 814 990, Mobiltel.: +387 63 999 706, E - Mail:
park@makarthoteli.com,
Source: Makart Hoteli d.o.o. Design and Programming: *„Morgojelo Hotel ****" * in Morgojelohotel.com 2008 under:
http://hotelmogorjelo.com/en/about_hotel/karaotok/ (retrieved on 28. March 2019).

Annotation: The hotel´s website states that it is a 4 - star hotel. According to the star - rating provided inside the hotel, it has, however, only 3 stars. The rates displayed in the hotel, also differ from those on the website.[181]

181

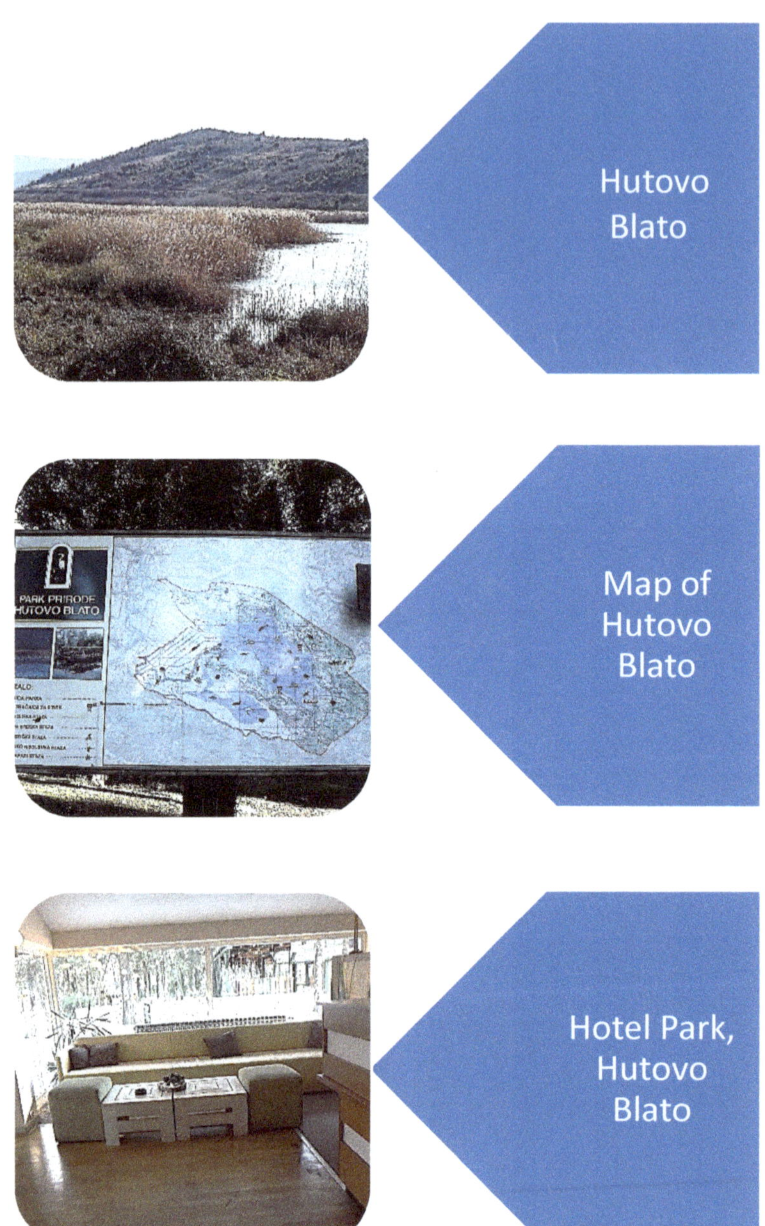

Hutovo
Blato

Map of
Hutovo
Blato

Hotel Park,
Hutovo
Blato

10.   Prehistoric grave stelai and the village Paoča

In the surrounding area of Medjugorje one can visit many prehistoric grave stelai and cumuli.from the 12th century. The stelai stem, for the most, from the time of the Turkish occupation. Special locations for these stelai are Medjugorje, Vionica und Ljubuski.[182] [183] Near Stolac, on the Vidovo polje plain, you can visit 133 of these stelai from the 15th and 16th century.[184] [185] In Paoča you can not only admire the stelai, but also visit the "workplace" of the Franciscan monk, Father Didak Bunti, who was important for the region. [186]

11.   Die Vjetrenica - Grotto

On route to Dubrovnik, about 75 km from Medjugorje, lies the Vjetrenica - Grotto, which extends over 6 km.[187]

---

[182] Franjo Sušac (Text und Foto), Conect Mostar (und Design), *Medjugorje MONOGRAFIA PER I PELLEGRINI,* Grafotisak, Grude 2014, page 6.
[183] arheoportal: „Hercegovački arheološki portal" in: Portale Archaeologicum Herzegoviae 18. September 2016, under:
https://arheohercegovina.com/2016/09/18/humski-bilizi-i-unesco/ (retrieved on 16 September 2019).
[184] Franjo Sušac (Text und Foto), Conect Mostar (und Design), *Medjugorje MONOGRAFIA PER I PELLEGRINI,* Grafotisak, Grude 2014, page 70.
[185] Komisija/Povjerenstvo za očuvanje nacionalnih spomenika - Комисија за очување националних споменика: „Standing Tombstones – UNESCO" 27. April 2016, under:
https://www.youtube.com/watch?v=mOTv9M6TxVU (retrieved on 16 September 2019).
[186] Franjo Sušac (Text und Foto), Conect Mostar (und Design), *Medjugorje MONOGRAFIA PER I PELLEGRINI,* Grafotisak, Grude 2014, page 11.
[187] Medjugorje Hotel & Spa: *„Surroundings of Medjugorje Natural Wonders And Cultural Attractions"* in: Medjugorje Hotel & Spa 2017, under:
https://www.medjugorjehotelspa.com/en/medjugorje-what-to-see-in-the-surroundings/ (retrieved on 28 March 2019).

12.   Tito´s Bunker in Konij[188]

This bunker, in which 4,6 billion US dollars were invested, was top secret. Today it is open to tourists. It is located below the Zlatar mountain at a depth of 280 meters. The bunker consists of 100 rooms and could have provided shelter for about 350 people for up to 6 months. More information can be found on the following website: http://www.visitkonjic.com (retrieved on 1 July 2019).

13.   River - Rafting on the Neretva River

For water lovers, the Neretva River offers an 18 km long river - rafting route in the summer. In winter, the route is shortened to 7 km.[189] The rafting route is usually from Glavatičevo to Džajići. The tour lasts on average 5 hours.[190] If you are interested, you should contact the rafting club in Konjic.[191]. More information can be found on the following wesite: http://www.visitkonjic.com. (retrieved on 1 July 2019).

---

[188] Marko Plesnšnik, *Bosnien und Herzegowina, 6. Aufl.,* Trescher Verlag, 10117 Berlin 2017, page 259.

[189] Medjugorje Hotel & Spa: „*Surroundings of Medjugorje Natural Wonders And Cultural Attractions*" in: Medjugorje Hotel & Spa 2017, under: https://www.medjugorjehotelspa.com/en/medjugorje-what-to-see-in-the-surroundings/ (retrieved on 28 March 2019).

[190] Amel Salihbasić, „*Komm, entdecke, erzähle weiter BOSNIEN UND HERZEGOWINA 30 unvergessliche Tage*", 3. Ed.., Amel Salihbasić (self - publishing), Vienna, Austria 2017, page 9.

[191] Amel Salihbasić, „*Komm, entdecke, erzähle weiter BOSNIEN UND HERZEGOWINA 30 unvergessliche Tage*", 3. Ed., Amel Salihbasić (self - publishing), Vienna, Austria 2017, page 9.

MATTERS WORTH KNOWING

1.   The Parish Office of St. James

Gospin trg 1, 88266 Medjugorje, Bosnia and Herzegovina
Tel: +387-36-653-300 / Fax: + 387 36-653-360
E-mail: ured@medjugorje.hr

2.   Information Centre "MIR"
s
The Information Centre is located to the side of St. James
Church.

The opening hours are:
Weekdays: 08.00 am – 6.00 pm
Sundays: 09.00 am – 2.00 pm

Tel: +387-36-651-999/E-mail:
seminar.marija@medjugorje.hr

3.   The Information Desk:

Tel: + 387-36-653-316
E - mail: informacije@medjugorje.hr

4.   Translation of the Holy Mass by radio:

The Holy Masses at St. James Church are simultaneously
translated into different languages. To enjoy a translation,
you either need a small radio with headphones or a
smartphone. During "peak" pilgrim times, radios can also be
bought or rented from the "KIOSK" next to the Hall of the
Blessed John Paul II. Many souvenir shops also have
inexpensive radios for sale. Each language has its own radio
frequency. The necessary radio frequency to follow the Holy

Mass in your native language, is stated on the Information Centre´s information brochure.

5.　　Radio „MIR" Medjugorje

Tel: +387-36-653-580 /Fax: + 387-36-653-552
E - mail: radio-mir@medjugorje.hr

6.　　Bookshops "MIR"

There are two "MIR" book-/souvenir shops. The first, is right next to the Information Centre. The second, is slightly offset from the Information Centre towards the Church.

Annotation: When business is slow, the shops can also close before the signposted closing time.

7.　　Bookshop "Les Editions Sakramento"

The predominantly French - speaking bookshop is located near the Garden of St. Francis.

Website: https://sakramento.com/ (retrieved on 1 July 2019).

8.   The German - Christian Bookshop "Tiberias"

In this bookshop, German is spoken. This well - stocked bookshop, also has an online shop.

Christliche Buchhandlung TIBERIAS
Robert Teisler
P.BOX 23,
Medjugorje, 88266,
Bosnia and Herzegovina
E - mail: tiberias.medjugorje@*gmail.com*
Tel.: 00387 – (0) 36655007
Fax: 00387 – (0) 36655007
http://www.tiberiasmedjugorje.com [192]

---

[192] TIBERIAS unter: http://tiberiasmedjugorje.com/index.php/de-DE/kontakt (retrieved on 20 May 2019).

9. International Book-, Souvenir Shop „Devotions"

This book- and souvenir shop also carries rare books. The shop is located in Papa Ivana II Street. Starting off at St. James Church, it is on the right - hand side when walking towards the main post office.

The corresponding address is that of the Pension "Devotions" and not of the bookshop:

Devotions d.o.o.
Kristine 26,
88266 Medjugorje
Bosnia and Herzegovina
Tel./Fax: ++387 (36) 651 -497
devotions@tel.net.ba
www.medjugorje-devotions.com

10. Medical Services

In direct vicinity of St. James Church, is a First Aid Station run by the Maltese relief organisation. Unfortunately, this station is CLOSED from 31 October until 14 January.

In case of emergency, one is asked to dial: 124

or alternatively, to contact the First Aid branch in Čitluk:
+ 387 (0) 36641040.

11.　Pharmacies (Ljekarna)

In the centre of Medjugorje are several well - stocked pharmacies: Two of them are:

1. **Biopharm Pharmacy**
   Pape Ivana II
   Međugorje 88260,

Tel.: +387 36 651-841

2. **Lubina Pharmacy**
   Franjevačkih mučenika 61,
   Međugorje 88260,

   Tel.: +387 36 805-148

12.   Bus Station

In Dr. Franje Tuđmana street, directly next to the main post
- office, is the long distance bus station.
From here, buses also leave for Sarajevo and Zagreb.
(Tel.: +387 651 393)

13.   Taxis:

The taxi rank is in front of St. James Church in Pape Ivana
Paula II Street. Unfortunately, the taxi drivers' knowledge of
foreign languages is very limited. The drivers are also in a
hurry. In my case, I was treated very courteously, but the
driver didn´t know the Dervish Tekke personally. So, he
showed me another church as the monastery. It is also
worthwhile to agree on the length of the stay at the
destination before departure. If not, there may be surcharges
and unnecessary quarrels.

Taxi Rates:

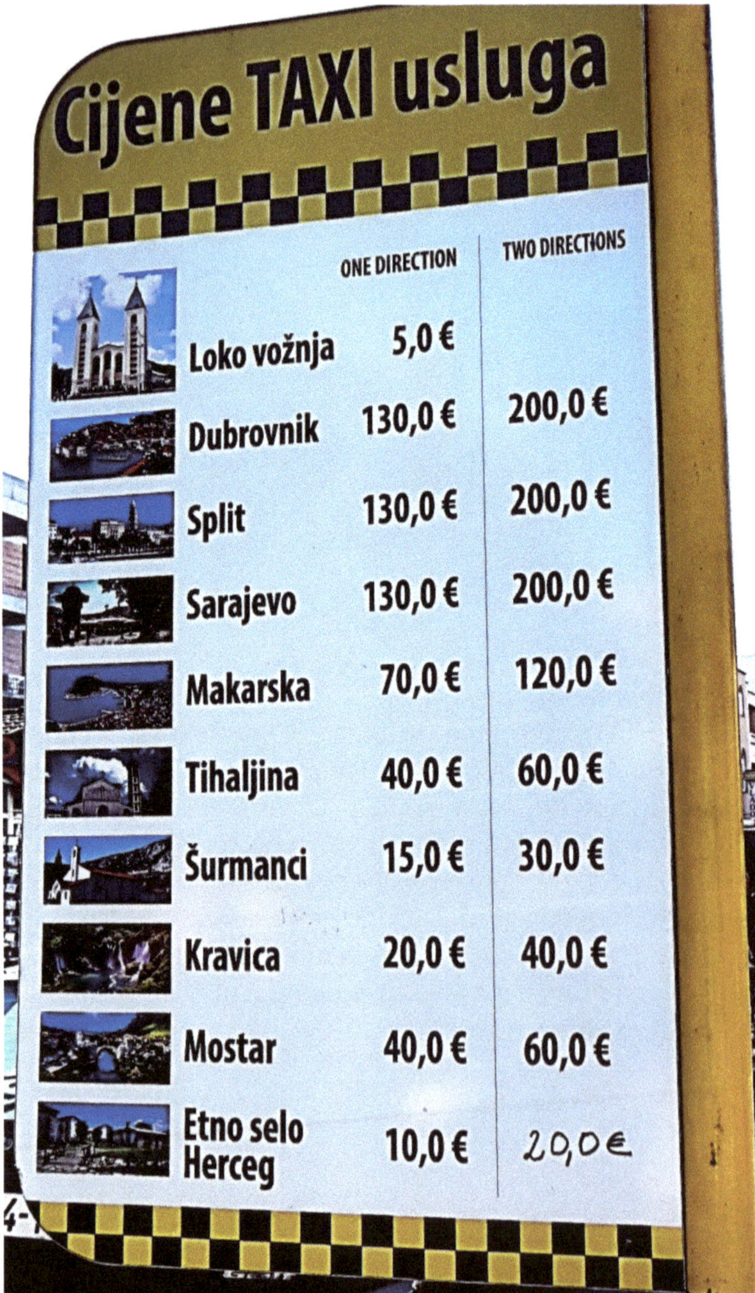

Cijene TAXI usluga
ONE DIRECTION
TWO DIRECTIONS
Loko vožnja
5,0 €
Dubrovnik
130,0 €
200,0 €
Split
130,0 €
200,0 €
Sarajevo
130,0 €
200,0 €
Makarska
70,0 €
120,0 €
Tihaljina
40,0 €
60,0 €
Šurmanci
15,0 €
30,0 €
Kravica
20,0 €
40,0 €
Mostar
40,0 €
60,0 €
Etno selo Herceg
10,0 €
20,0 €

14.   Organised excursions

a)   Pax Travel

The Agency is based in the Medjugorje Hotel & Spa Hotel and offers organised excursions.

Pax Travel:[193]
Ulica fra Slavka Bararića 29,
Medjugorje (BiH)
Tel: + 387 036 640 456
E - mail:
info@pax-travel.com
booking@pax-travel.com
Web: www.pax-travel.com
Skype:
pax.travel1
Whatsapp:
Tel.: +387 63 451 521

b)   Nicola Travel d. o. o.

Surmanci Medjugorje
Tel.: 00387 63 359 104
Nicola.surmanci90@gmail.com

15.   Shopping:

On route to Čitluk, as part of Hotel Herceg, there is a **"dm"** drugstore.
In Čitluk itself, there is a well – assorted smaller shopping centre with a Café, hair - dresser and filling - station: the **"Konzum"**.
Right next to Hotel Herceg Etno Selo, there is another shopping mall with café and play - corner, the so - called **"Park & Shop"**.

---

[193] Pax travel Medjugorje, Informationsbrochure

16.   Post Offices:

There are two post offices in Medjugorje.
The main post office is in Dr. Franje Tuđmana Street.
Should the local map be sold out at the Information Centre,
one can also get it here.
As far customer service is concerned, that is a matter of
luck. Some clerks are more motivated, others less. Thus, it
can happen that some employees are no longer prepared to
carry out more complex tasks half an hour before closing
time.
The 2nd post office is right next to the bookstore "MIR". On
Saturdays this branch is even open until 3:00 p.m. . But
more complex mailings are not sent off from there.

Unfortunately, honey, alcohol and food supplies may not be sent by post. (Tel.: +387 651 990)

17.   Parking Lot:

There is a large gravel parking lot behind St. James Church.
Yet, on special occasions, you should be early, in order to
park there. Unfortunately, it is not illuminated at night.

18.   Miracles of the Sun: Caution!!!

Although real miracles of the sun are supposed to occur in
Medjugorje, nevertheless, pay attention to your vision. Even
though a real sun miracle should not hurt your eyes, there
can also be phenomena, which merely resemble a miracle of
the sun. Also, the sun in Bosnia and Herzegovina, is quite
strong. Unprotected looking at the sun can cause permanent
damage (e.g. solar retinopathy) or even blindness. For the
right protection of your eyes, you may want to consult an
eye doctor before starting your journey.

19.   Restaurants

There are several good restaurants in Medjugorje. If one
wants to try something different, there is the "Ventum", not
far from the shopping centre Park & Ride.

20. Fasting

If you want to fast with bread and water, you can get bread in almost every supermarket. You can get a better quality of bread from the Pekarna (bakery). Please seek medical advice, however, before going on a fast, in order to avoid any nutritional deficiencies.

21. Confessing in your mother tongue

Maybe you go to confession regularly, but maybe not. Many people say: "Oh, God knows that I'm sorry anyway!" Well, the monthly confession is a request of the Mother of God and think about it, if you can't bring yourself to go to

confession after all. I would say, it could have an unexpectedly positive effect on your pilgrimage experience. The priests and Franciscan friars who administer the sacrament are working with astonishingly untiring dedication. On special occasions, they may even hear your confessions until 1:00 a.m.. Unfortunately, it is not always possible to IMMEDIATELY find a priest to confess to in one's mother tongue. My recommendation: ask the friars. Most friars tend to speak additional languages. The friars' confessionals are on the side of the Candle Park.
As a last resort, the Information Centre can mediate. If you have forgotten how to confess, the priest will most certainly be happy to guide you through the confession.

22.   Donations

The parish of Medjugorje does not publicly ask for donations. Nevertheless, it will certainly appreciate a donation, which can be handed in at the parish office.

23.   Registration of Pilgrim Groups

Every pilgrim group has to register with the Information Centre.

24.   Hotels

Medjugorje has hotels for every budget and taste. Guest houses include the Villa Gaga and Pansion Becun.
There are the following 3 - star hotels: Hotel Speranza (directly opposite of Apparition Hill), Hotel Barbarić and Hotel Ivona.
The 4 - star Medjugorje Hotel & Spa Hotel is comfortable but kept simple. Other 4 - star hotels are the Hotel Leone, Hotel Luna, Hotel Wojtyla, Hotel Klemo, Hotel Herceg and the Aparthotel Irish House.

Hotel Speranza

Hotel Barbarić

Medju-
gorje
Hotel &
Spa

Hotel
Leone

Hotel
Luna

Hotel
Wojtyla

Hotel
Klemo

Hotel
Herceg

25.   Human Outlook

Finally, I would like to ask you not to be put off by the many souvenir shops. Nor should one assume that every pilgrim is now an angel with the perfect manners. But the majority of people strive for an unusually humane, supportive and patient interaction. Also, you might (not) be bothered by the attitude of a clergyman, at times. We are all human beings and don´t know about the inner workings of a person. A certain hegemony of Italian pilgrims is striking, which results in a preference for the Italian language. Some people might find this troubling. But, let´s think about it; it is only natural to be orientated towards the majority of your guests. Don´t be troubled by earthly matters, but rather follow the invitation of the Blessed Mother and through Our Lady´s help, seek to encounter Our Lord here.

.

26.   Site plan

ŽUPA SV. JAKOVA- SREDIŠNJI MOLITVENI PROSTOR
LEGENDA
1- ŽUPNA CRKVA
2- VANJSKI OLTAR
3- KAPELICA KLANJANJA
4- ISPOVJEDAONICE
5- KIP KRALJICE MIRA
6- DVORANA BLAŽENOG IVANA PAVLA II.
7- KIP USKRSLOG SPASITELJA I
POSTAJE KRIŽNOG PUTA
8- KRUNICA OTAJSTVA SVJETLA
9- RASPELO- MJESTO MOLITVE I
PALJENJA SVIJEĆA
10- KIP SV. LEOPOLDA MANDIĆA
11- ŽUPNI URED
12- URED INFORMACIJA
13- SUVENIRNICA
14- POŠTA / TELEFON
11- PROSTOR ZA ODMOR HODOČASNIKA
16- WC
17- AMBULANTA PRVE POMOĆI
18- RADIOPOSTAJA "MIR" MEĐUGORJE
19- PARKIRALIŠTE
20- GROBLJE KOVAČICA

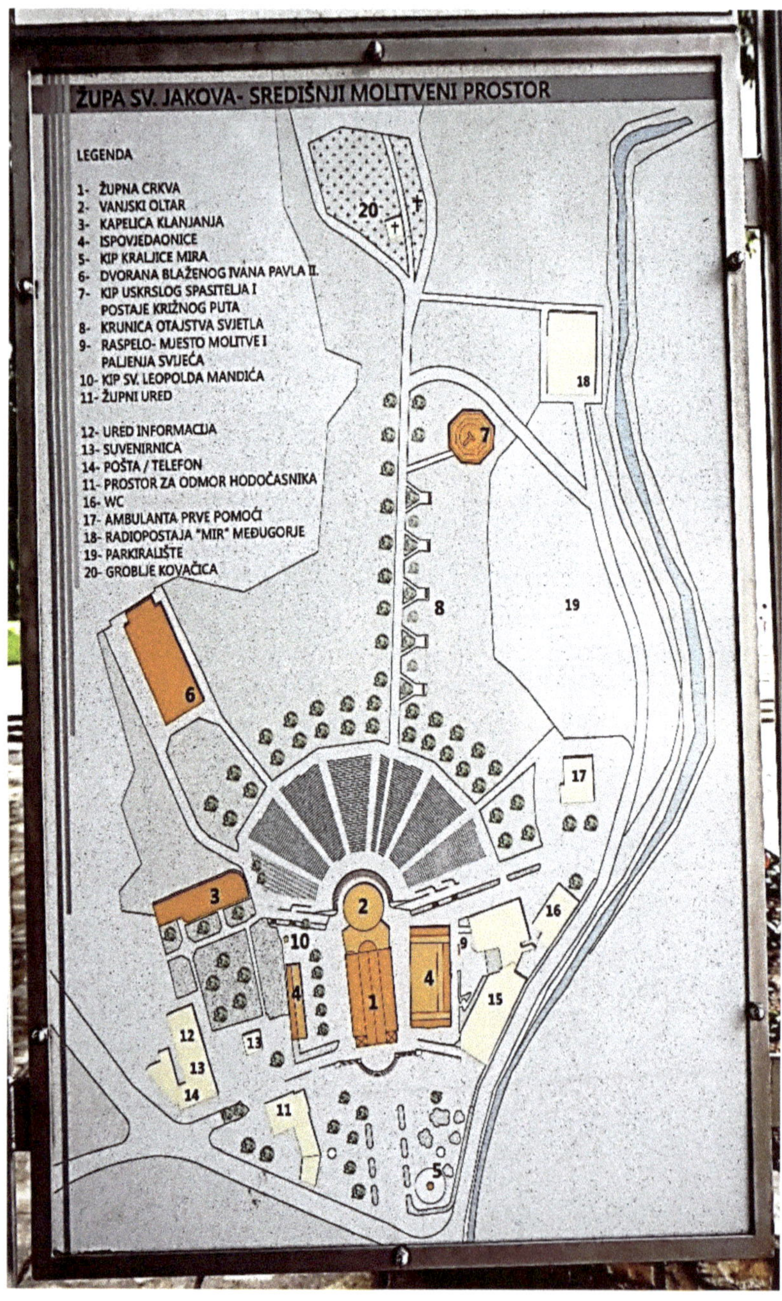

1. St. James Church
2. Outdoor Altar
3. Adoration Chapel
4. Confessionals
5. Statue of the Queen of Peace
6. Hall of the Blessed John Paul IIaul II
7. Statue of the Risen Christ – Stations of the Cross
8. The Luminous Mysteries of the Rosary
9. Crucifix – Prayer Ground – Votive Candles
10. Statue of St. Leopold Mandić
11. Parish Office
12. Information Centre
13. Souvenir shops
14. Postal Services/Telephone
15. Outdoor Lounge
16. Toilets
17. First Aid Station
18. Radio „Mir" Medjugorje
19. Parking lot
20. Kovaćica Cemetary

27. Local Map

MEDJUGORJE
Križevac
(Cross Mountain)
The Stations of the Cross
i Čilići
Fra Joze Vasilja
Put Križevaca
Parking Lot
Cenacolo
Fra Vendelina Vasilja
Parking Lot
Sege
Podbrdo
(Apparition Hill)
Podbrdo
3. Entrance
2. Entrance
Podbrdo
1. Entrance
(Blue Cross)
Put Kovačici
Cemetery
Kraljice Mira
Pharmacy
Frankjevackih mucenica
Kiosk
Via Domini
Statue of the Risen Christ
Parking Lot
Bijakovići
Post - Office
Info
St. James
Fra Slavka
Barbarića
Fra Slavka Barbarića
Il ejned
First Aid
Taxi Rank
Pape Ivana
Mary's Meals
Kralja Tomislava
Pharmacy
Kardinala Alojzije Stepinac
Post - Office
Bus Station